Comments on other *Amazing Stories* from readers & reviewers

"*You might call them the non-fiction response to Harlequin romances: easy to consume and potentially addictive.*"
Robert Martin, *The Chronicle Herald*

"*Tightly written volumes filled with lots of wit and humour about famous and infamous Canadians.*"
Eric Shackleton, *The Globe and Mail*

"*This is popular history as it should be... For this price, buy two and give one to a friend.*"
Terry Cook, a reader from Ottawa, on **Rebel Women**

"*Stories are rich in description, and bristle with a clever, stylish realness.*"
Mark Weber, *Central Alberta Advisor*, on **Ghost Town Stories II**

"*The resulting book is one readers will want to share with all the women in their lives.*"
Lynn Martel, *Rocky Mountain Outlook*, on **Women Explorers**

"[The books are] *long on plot and character and short on the sort of technical analysis that can be dreary for all but the most committed academic.*"
Robert Martin, *The Chronicle Herald*

"*A compelling read. Bertin...has selected only the most intriguing tales, which she narrates with a wealth of detail.*"
Joyce Glasner, *New Brunswick Reader*, on **Strange Events**

"*The heightened sense of drama and intrigue, combined with a good dose of human interest is what sets* Amazing Stories *apart.*"
Pamela Klaffke, *Calgary Herald*

UNBELIEVABLE CANADIAN WAR STORIES

AMAZING STORIES®

UNBELIEVABLE CANADIAN WAR STORIES

Well Beyond the Call of Duty

MILITARY

by Pat MacAdam

To Janet, my loving wife and my literary Whip,
who took the blows while I did it my way.

PUBLISHED BY ALTITUDE PUBLISHING CANADA LTD.
1500 Railway Avenue, Canmore, Alberta T1W 1P6
www.altitudepublishing.com
www.amazingstories.ca
1-800-957-6888

Extreme care has been taken to ensure that all information presented in
this book is accurate and up to date. Neither the author nor the
publisher can be held responsible for any errors.

Publisher	Stephen Hutchings
Series Editor	Diana Marshall
Editor	Gayl Veinotte
Cover and Layout	Bryan Pezzi

We acknowledge the financial support of the Government
of Canada through the Book Publishing Industry Development
Program (BPIDP) for our publishing activities.

Altitude GreenTree Program
Altitude Publishing will plant twice as many trees as were used
in the manufacturing of this product.

Library and Archives Canada Cataloguing in Publication

Macadam, Pat
    Unbelievable Canadian war stories / Pat MacAdam.

(Amazing stories)
Includes bibliographical references.
ISBN 1-55439-051-6

    1. World War, 1939-1945--Canada. I. Title.
II. Series: Amazing stories (Canmore, Alta.)

D768.15.M3159 2006   940.53'71   C2006-900803-5

Amazing Stories® is a registered trademark of Altitude Publishing Canada Ltd.

Printed and bound in Canada by Friesens
2 4 6 8 9 7 5 3 1

Contents

Foreword

Readers of my *Sun Media* newspaper columns ask me why I write about war more than any other subject. My answer is, I don't write about war. I write about its participants — Canadian heroes who put their lives on the line in defence of our liberty and freedom and our quality of life. Many of them have never had their incredible stories told, and these stories ought to be preserved for posterity.

I was a guest speaker at a meeting of a historical society in my hometown of Glace Bay, Nova Scotia. I asked my audience of 100 if anyone had ever heard of David Romans. None had.

Flying Officer David Romans was the first Nova Scotian to be awarded the Distinguished Flying Cross from King George VI at Buckingham Palace. He was killed when his Flying Fortress was shot down on a bomb run to sink the *Admiral Scheer* in a Norwegian fjord. David Romans had 58 bombing sorties over Germany. He was just 20 years old when he died. David Romans was from Glace Bay, and forgotten.

My father was a gunner with three stripes and a crown in World War I. He didn't like to talk about it, because it was too horrible. One day, a German shell dropped into his battery and killed everyone except him. He was spared because he was standing behind his horse. The horse was killed and pieces of shrapnel passed under its belly and into my father's legs.

For the next 45 years, the Department of Veterans Affairs sent my father a return Glace Bay–Halifax–Glace Bay bus ticket for Camp Hill Hospital. Doctors continued to pick out pieces of metal. The last count, before he died, was 140 shards of shrapnel.

Canadians have never started a war, but when liberty and freedom came under attack they were always first among volunteers to fight the aggressor. It is not my intention to popularize war — the brutality, the killings, the atrocities, and the senseless loss of life. But, from time to time, wars do break out and some Canadian men and women serve above and beyond the call of duty. These are the heroes whose stories must be told.

PAT MACADAM

Prologue

Royal Canadian Air Force (RCAF) Spitfire pilot Keith "Skeets" Ogilvie waited shivering in the cold and dark of a March night in 1944 to make his bid for freedom from Stalag Luft 111 in Sagan, 161 kilometres southeast of Berlin. Snow still crusted the ground, and the temperature was below freezing. The pilot's nerves were on edge as he watched the prisoners ahead of him shuffle through the tunnel, code-named "Harry," one of three escape tunnels designed by Canadian Flight Lieutenant Wally Floody. The prisoners passed in front of Skeets ... 72, 73, 74 ... He remembered that Floody had been unexpectedly transferred to another camp the previous night, and his thoughts drifted for a moment ... 74, 75 ...

Number 75! It was his turn! He crouched down and inched his way slowly through the dark, dank tunnel, trying desperately to control his breathing. Empty jam tins had been telescoped together and periodically positioned along the tunnel to make ventilation pipes. As he emerged from the tunnel, a shout stopped him cold. The German guards had seen the steam rising from the escape hole outside the wire. Gunfire shattered the night. In a sudden moment, Skeets's hopes and dreams were dashed.

The flying ace was recaptured almost immediately, as

were 73 of the 75 escapees. Soon after, 50 of the would-be escapees were executed by firing squad in nearby woods. Skeets Ogilvie's name was not on that list of 50, and he went through life wondering why he had been spared.

* * *

Keith "Skeets" Ogilvie was awarded the Distinguished Flying Cross (DFC). After the war, he stayed in the RCAF and served as a squadron leader in Trenton, Centralia, Rockcliffe, and Downsview. He retired in April 1962 and passed away May 26, 1998.

Chapter 1
Was George
Beurling Murdered?

W as George Beurling, Canada's highest scoring World War II fighter ace, murdered?

I believe he was and I set out to prove it. I checked my trap lines in Ottawa, Washington, London, Tel Aviv, Haifa, Montreal, Old Chelsea in Quebec, South Woodslee in Ontario, New York, and Rome.

I spoke with Syd Shulemson, Canada's most decorated Jewish fighter pilot and the man who recruited Beurling to fly for Israel. I spoke with Israeli air attachés in various embassies. I spoke with Eddy Kaplansky who flew with the RCAF in WWII and the nascent Israeli air force. I spoke with fellow Spitfire pilots, Jerry Billing and Robert Hyndman. I spoke with and e-mailed former British Member of Parliament (MP) and espionage writer Nigel West and, last but not least,

I was in contact with General Meir Amit, a former head of Israel's Mossad spy agency. None had conclusive proof that Beurling's plane had been sabotaged, because any forensic evidence had been destroyed in a crash so hot it melted the plane's metal frame.

Months later, I received a single sheet of notepaper in a plain brown envelope. There was no signature. It was postmarked Tel Aviv. The mysterious communication re-ignited and added to the mystery surrounding the death of Canada's greatest fighter ace.

On the morning of 20 May, Beurling and Cohen had taken off from Rome's Urbe airfield to test Norseman NC79822. Witnesses reported seeing flames coming from its engine as it returned to land and, as it touched down, there was a thunderous explosion. It proved impossible for would-be rescuers to get near to the blazing wreck and both Beurling and Cohen perished in the flames.

Was it a simple accident, as suggested? Was it Arab sabotage, as rumoured?

There remains a further possibility. A Haganah (Jewish military group) operative in Rome suggested later that a British agent had been responsible for the crash. He claimed that the agent had been briefed to do whatever he could to prevent planes and volunteers from reaching Palestine. The Haganah agent added that, following the crash, the British agent was kidnapped and summarily executed. If correct, the agent had obviously exceeded his mandate but the truth will probably never be known.

I suspect the letter was from former Mossad chief, General Meir Amit.

The "official accident investigation" was actually an investigation by the Rome police. It was over in eight days. It concluded that the "fire was due to a backfire caused by the engulfment of the carburetor." We may never know if Beurling's plane was sabotaged.

A 2003 reprint of a minor classic of war in the air, *Canada's Fighting Pilots*, adds a new dimension to the 1948 death of Canada's greatest World War II ace. The book was written in 1965 by late CBC newsman, Ed Cosgrove. In it, Cosgrove maintains that Beurling died in Rome in the flaming wreckage of a surplus Canadian-built Norseman he was ferrying to Israel. Beurling and his co-pilot, Leonard Cohen, another World War II fighter pilot, were practising touch-and-go takeoffs and landings at Urbe airport. Just after the awkward Norseman took off, it staggered. Witnesses saw flames shooting along the belly of the plane and heard the engine cut out. Veteran pilots will tell you that a cardinal rule of flying is that, in the event of engine failure, the pilot should use what little flying speed he has to glide straight in. An attempt to bank results in a loss of power and altitude.

George Beurling broke the rule. He tried to turn the aircraft around and return to the field. Ed Cosgrove and Brik Billing believe he sacrificed his life because the doomed plane was headed straight for heavily populated tenement buildings. Others think his control cables may have been burned up.

The Norseman stalled and dropped like a stone. When rescue crew arrived on the scene the metal from the plane was running along the ground like mercury. The bodies of George Beurling and Leonard Cohen were charred beyond recognition.

Syd Shulemson, who lives in Montreal, is highly decorated (the Distinguished Service Order and a Distinguished Flying Cross, flying Beaufighters and Mosquitoes). He is convinced that Beurling's plane was sabotaged. For one thing, he maintains that both pilots were far too experienced to have attempted to bank a stalled, burning aircraft. Shulemson was also unaware that Beurling's flight path was on a heading with a densely populated neighbourhood. Both Shulemson and Eddy Kaplansky, a World War II RCAF flyer and an original Israeli air force veteran who now lives in Haifa, believe but cannot prove that a saboteur placed an oily rag under the exhaust manifold and turned the fabric covered aircraft into a flaming coffin. Shulemson says security around the Norseman planes parked at Urbe airfield was non-existent.

After the crash, no autopsies were conducted. The

official causes of death are still unknown: impact, fire, or suffocation. The bodies were so badly burned, it was not possible to determine who was flying the aircraft.

Eddie Kaplansky wrote more than 50 years later: "the fact is that the true cause of the crash remains unknown. There was never an official inquiry, neither by the Italian or Israeli authorities. As the five-day old State of Israel was engaged in a struggle for its existence, there were much more pressing things to worry about."

Syd Shulemson was one of Israel's main agents in North America. He was instrumental in putting a deal together for Israel to buy 15 Norseman planes for $12,500 each. Israel had an option to buy an additional seven. The United States had an embargo on supplying planes to Israel, but under their very eyes, Shulemson managed to secure a Flying Fortress bomber for the nascent Israeli air force.

Brik Billing's father, Jerry, flew with Beurling in Malta. Jerry flew more than 250 Spitfire sorties over Malta and Normandy.

"Beurling was on Malta long before me and flew a lot more sorties than I flew. We flew sorties. The Americans flew missions. Missions sounded too evangelical for us." Jerry Billing also subscribes to the sabotage theory. "It would be so easy to stuff an oily rag under the exhaust manifold. Or, a pin-prick in the gas line would force atomized gas out under pressure as a mist and it would ignite explosively."

Jerry Billing is also on the record as stating that

Beurling's death could have been an act of Italian revenge. "Remember," he says, "Beurling shot down a lot of Italian planes over Malta and killed a lot of Italian pilots. He was a deadly shot and he didn't waste his ammunition. He boasted openly about shooting an Italian pilot in the head and seeing blood streaming down the fuselage. The incident gave him nightmares for years afterwards."

Beurling was Canada's leading fighter ace with 31 kills and a share of a 32nd. In a span of 14 days he shot down 27 enemy planes. Beurling was the very first warrior to be awarded four gallantry medals by the king at an investiture at Buckingham Palace. He was awarded the Distinguished Service Order, a Distinguished Flying Cross, and a Distinguished Flying Medal and Bar.

George Beurling has gone down in history as "Buzz" Beurling, but Jerry Billing remembers the people who flew with him never referred to him "as anything else but George or Beurl. George was extremely shy and introverted and would rather let a comment stand than correct it. The RAF's [Royal Air Force] 'Laddie' Lucas called him 'Screwball,' but Lucas never knew Beurling before Malta, and they were hardly close friends. The nickname 'Buzz' was a pure invention of the RCAF public relations machine. It wouldn't do to have Canada's leading air ace nicknamed Screwball."

Only people who knew Beurling called him by his given name. Brik Billing adds: "My father tells me it became an acid test for him. If a person called out 'Buzz' or 'Screwball,' Beurling knew automatically that they were not known friends."

George Beurling was only 21 when he dominated the skies over Malta. He was a fearless warrior and survived nine crashes or bailouts. Those who knew him maintain that ice water flowed through his veins. In the air, he was a stone killer. He had perfected the art of deflection shooting on his days off at the Malta dump, taking out rats and lizards with his .38 revolver. His brain rapidly calculated where a plane would be in a second or two, and that's where his bullets would be, too.

A Spitfire's wing guns had enough firepower for just 15 seconds. Beurling rationed his "squirts" to two or three seconds. After one sortie, he returned and claimed a probable kill. He said he had fired a five-round burst into the cockpit of an Italian aircraft and described exactly where the bullets had struck home. Cosgrove's book records that "shortly afterwards, a report came through that an Italian aircraft had crashed during a raid that day. Investigation revealed five cannon holes, just where Beurling had described them."

Beurling was an unconventional loner. He was a sergeant pilot and resisted promotion until he was ordered to accept a commission. Sergeant Beurling may well have been "put up" for a Victoria Cross had he been a more conventional hero who didn't go out of his way to alienate the brass. He had few friends because most had been killed in the defence of Malta. Two of his best friends were Flight Sergeant Jean Paradis from Shawinigan and RAF pilot Eric "Heather"

Heatherington. Paradis died attacking a formation of over 20 bombers with fighter escorts. His last transmission was: "I see the bombers. I go there." Heatherington was killed in a Liberator crash off Gibraltar.

When the war was over, Beurling was only 23 and a lost soul. He tried selling life insurance in Montreal, but quit when he didn't sell a single policy in three months. Beurling barnstormed in air shows and country fairs in his personal Tiger Moth. His flying skills were extraordinary. During a lull in the blitz of Malta, Allied soldiers and airmen paraded down the main streets of Valetta in a morale boosting show of strength for the civilian population. Beurling flew one of three Spitfires at rooftop level. The planes flew so low that people on balconies looked down on the pilots. Beurling, however, wasn't satisfied with tame low-level flying. He flew down Valetta's main street, about 15 metres off the deck, upside down. His superiors were not amused.

After the war, Beurling tried to sign up with Chiang Kai-shek's Nationalist Air Force in China, but the Canadian government denied his application for a visa. In 1948, Syd Shulemson recruited him to fly for Israel:

"I told him there would be no pay, no rank, probably no uniform, and probably no Spitfire. The only pay he would receive would be that of an officer in the Israeli air force."

Spit and polish were never high on Beurling's priorities. His boots were never polished and he wore grungy Desert Rats' shorts and a cast-off New Zealand air force tunic.

Was George Beurling Murdered?

Syd Shulemson remembers:

Israel was brand new, and the Israelis may now deny it, but security was not as good as it should have been. I worked my contacts and told them to guard against an Arab attempt to assassinate Beurling. I told our New York agents that, when he arrived, he was to be put on the first available flight to Italy. But Beurling decided to spend a few days in New York and, publicity conscious that he was, he told the press where he was headed. The Arabs knew he was in New York and they knew his next stop was Rome.

Eddy Kaplansky says, "Israel's man in Rome probably didn't fully understand the dangers involved or, otherwise, he would not have used a top league fighter pilot for a simple ferrying job."

Brik Billing's postscript is: "Personally, I agree with Syd about the sabotage angle. Beurling on his own was a formidable adversary. If he had the chance to pass on his skills to a new crop of pilots, well, that's reason for sabotage right there."

The Canadian government ignored the death of Canada's greatest hero because of the political implications of Beurling's involvement in the Palestine question. The lone entry in the External Affairs telex traffic between Rome and Ottawa concerned payment for Beurling's funeral expenses. The cheap funeral Canada paid for never took place. Beurling was thought to have been buried in Rome's Verano Catholic cemetery.

Beurling's lady friend, Vivi Stokes, travelled to Rome to visit the grave of her lover. She was outraged when she learned his coffin had not been interred but, instead, was stored in a dingy warehouse waiting to be claimed. She arranged for his remains to be buried in a graveyard in Rome between the graves of Keats and Shelley. A funeral coach, drawn by two black stallions, carried his remains through the streets of Rome.

Beurling's family, followers of an offshoot of the Plymouth Brethren, was appalled that their son was laid to rest in "the ungodly city of Rome." Syd Shulemson was given permission to have the coffin exhumed and taken to Israel for burial. Beurling's coffin was flown to Haifa in a military plane. His casket lay in state covered with an Israeli flag, and an honour guard stood watch, resting on their arms reversed. As the funeral cortege wound its way through the streets of Haifa, Israeli warplanes streaked low overhead.

Beurling and Leonard Cohen were both buried in Haifa's Zabal cemetery near the cave of Elijah the Prophet. His simple gravestone carries only his name, rank, and serial number.

Chapter 2
Rogue Waves

F lying shotgun off Cape Farewell, Greenland, in December 1942, a Royal Air Force bomber pilot captured a one-in-a-billion photograph. The luxury liner turned troop ship, the *Queen Mary*, was on her side after being hit by a fluke "rogue wave."

Master Mariner Captain John Shaw, Sydney, says: "No one on board thought she would right herself. Had she gone over one more degree — just five inches [13 cm] — the *Queen Mary* would have capsized with 11,339 passengers and crew perishing in the frigid waters. It would have been the worst tragedy of our lifetime — the greatest sea disaster of all time."

Rogue waves are unpredictable and savagely destructive freaks of nature. They happen when fierce storm waves collide with currents running in the opposite direction. Waves 30 metres or higher are not uncommon. Superstitious seamen call them "holes in the ocean." These "holes" are actually deep troughs that precede the steep sheets of water.

The *Mary* was eastbound to Europe on voyage WW #19E carrying 10,389 Canadian and U.S. servicemen and a crew of 950. One of the largest ships afloat, she was also the fastest and could have carried the *Titanic* in her hold with more than 40 metres to spare. At 1,019 feet long, she was as long as three football fields. Her flank speed was 32 knots. The rogue wave completely engulfed the fore part and bridge and rose two-thirds the way up the 56-metre funnel. Thrown on her side, she listed almost 45 degrees to starboard. The force of the wave treated her as just another ocean-going ping-pong ball. Wartime censorship made sure "the incident never happened." Cunard-White Star Lines' records make no mention of the wave. Likewise, logs show only that the liner spent six weeks in dry dock while repairs were carried out around the clock to restore her to service. Neither shipping company nor military records reveal if anyone was swept overboard or if any of the 11,339 on board were killed or injured. The fore part of the ship, however, was set down 15 centimetres from the main deck. Lifeboats, davits, and ventilators were swept away. The galleys and food lockers were left in shambles.

The *Mary* and her sister ship, the *Queen Elizabeth*, played key roles in winning the war. Between them, they ferried two and a half million fighting troops. Returning to New

York, they were never deadheaded empty. They often carried 5,000 to 6,000 German prisoners of war to internment camps in Canada and the United States. To prepare them for war, the sisters were painted a dull, battleship grey. Their portholes were blacked out. Across the shipping lanes they were known as the Gray Ghosts or the Gray Ladies.

The *Mary* logged 966 kilometres on the New York–Boston–Halifax–England run. Zigzagging at 28 to 32 knots, she could outrun any ship or U-boat Germany could throw at her. Hitler put a price on her head: a reward of $250,000, an Iron Cross with Oak Leaves, and a hero's reception in Berlin to the U-boat captain who could sink her. With the power of 160,000 horses in her engine room, she provided scant opportunity for eager wolf-pack bounty hunters. Because of her great speed, she crossed the ocean unescorted. Her greatest danger points were the headlands off Ireland, Iceland, Greenland, and Canada's east coast where the wolf packs lay in wait. She received sea and air escort protection in those areas.

When the *Mary* was requisitioned as a troop ship, her luxurious fittings — several kilometres of carpeting, expensive art deco furniture and 200 containers of china, silver, and crystal — were removed and stored. Tiers of bunks, six high, were built in, and she could carry more than 16,000 on a single crossing. There were life rafts for only half that number.

Her log of July 30, 1943, contains this entry:

New York to Gourock [Clyde], 16,683 souls aboard. New York, 25 July, 1943. Gourock, 30 July, 1943. 3,353 miles [5,396 km], four days, 20 hours, 42 minutes. 28.73 knots. The greatest number of human beings ever embarked on one vessel.

The *Queen Mary* was the first ship to transport an entire armoured infantry division in a single crossing. She sailed under the Union Jack, but the U.S. military considered her one of their "ships of the Line" and, like all U.S. warships, she was "dry" except when Winston Churchill was on board. The British prime minister — code named Colonel Warden — made three wartime crossings with his daughter, Mary, and Brigadier Orde Wingate (on occasion Chindit commander), First Sea Lord Louis Mountbatten, and famed Dambuster squadron commander, Wing Commander Guy Gibson, V.C. The Chindit commander was a member of the Allied forces behind Japanese lines in Burma (now Myanmar).

Severe rationing was in effect in England, but not aboard the *Queen Mary*. Twice a day in six sittings of 2,000 each, soldiers could eat all they wanted and were encouraged to take cold cuts and sandwiches away for snacks during the day. Her vast food lockers held 400 tons of food: 70,307 kilograms of meat, 9,707 kilograms of ham and bacon, 8,000 jars of jam, 14,243 kilograms of canned fruit, 24,313 kilograms of butter, powdered eggs, and milk, 200,000 eggs, 60,000 cartons of ice cream, and 13,154 kilograms of fresh fruit. To slice enough ham, the slicing machines were started up in New York and operated non-stop throughout the entire voyage. Every morning there were 30,000 fresh eggs to go with the ham.

Initially, she carried only puny Lewis and Vickers machine guns and one 10-centimetre deck gun. Subsequently, she was fitted with Oerlikons guns and rockets, but none was ever fired in anger. She also was equipped with one of Britain's very early, very few, and very secret marine radar units.

Even though she gave German U-boats the slip, her war was not without mishap. In 1942, off the northwest coast of Ireland, she was joined by Royal Navy escorts, the 4,200-ton cruiser HMS *Curacao* and four destroyers. All ships sailed at flank speed in prescribed zigzag courses.

The *Curacao* zigged when she should have zagged and the *Queen Mary* cut through 8 centimetres of "armour plate like a knife through butter." Her bow was guillotine sharp and had been especially strengthened for collisions or icebergs. Horrified watchers on deck saw halves of the *Curacao* on either side. More than 335 British sailors died. The 81,237-ton *Queen Mary*, under strict orders not to stop or slow down, sailed on. Destroyer escorts picked up 72 survivors. Seventy tons of concrete were poured into the *Mary*'s bow for emergency repairs, and she had to make for Boston because there was no dry dock space anywhere in Britain.

After the war, she brought U.S. and Canadian servicemen back home. She also made 12 crossings carrying 12,886 war brides and children — and 10 stowaways. The retired *Queen*, 1,001 Atlantic crossings under her keel, is now at anchor in Long Beach, California, as a floating museum and major tourist attraction.

Paul Gallico, the highest paid magazine writer in the United States, may have been a passenger on the *Mary* when she was struck by the rogue wave. *Cosmopolitan* magazine had sent him off to Europe to be their war correspondent. Years later he wrote a best-selling book about a luxury liner that turned turtle in mid-ocean. Hollywood bought the film rights and it became a blockbuster movie called *The Poseidon Adventure*.

Chapter 3
Jake Warren,
Valleyfield Survivor

T hirty years after their frigate was torpedoed off Cape Race, Newfoundland, in 1944, two shipmates met accidentally in London. Irving Kaplan had been chief petty officer, signals yeoman, on the *Valleyfield*, which sank within minutes of being hit. He was attending a memorial service for the *Athabaskan*, a Canadian destroyer sunk by an E-boat in the English Channel on April 29, 1944.

The *Athabaskan*, the *Iroquois*, and the *Haida* had been sweeping the channel for U-boats and E-boats for weeks before D-Day. One of two torpedoes hit the *Athabaskan*'s magazine. The glow of her funeral fire was visible 48 kilometres away. She sank within 10 minutes: 128 died and 86 were captured.

Kaplan was inching along the receiving line when he heard a bellow: "YO!" (every yeoman was nicknamed "YO"). The bellow came from one of two officers who had survived the sinking of the *Valleyfield* — Lieutenant Jack "Jake" Hamilton Warren. Jake was Canada's high commissioner to Britain — the main man in the receiving line.

The *Valleyfield*'s life was short. She was a frigate, a stretch corvette (96 feet longer) powered by twin screws. Her top speed was 19 knots. The other surviving officer, Lieutenant Ian Tate, jokes that "the best she could do was 17 knots downhill." She was 301 feet long and weighed 1,445 tons. She was launched on July 17, 1943, and commissioned in December.

The *Valleyfield* made one overseas crossing. She was assigned to convoy escort duty to England, but was detached to assist the disabled *Dundee* to an Azores port. She then took the damaged *Mulgrave* under tow to Scotland. On April 27, 1944, the *Valleyfield* left Londonderry with a convoy to return to Canada. The crossing was uneventful. Five escorts handed the convoy over to a local escort group and made smoke for St. John's. Ian Tate remembers the *Valleyfield*'s heading: 002 North, 80 kilometres off Cape Race. The corvette's companions were the *Halifax*, the *Frontenac*, the *Giffard*, and the *Edmunston*. They sailed line abreast, about 4 kilometres apart, at 13 knots.

Tate also recalls that they did not follow evasive zigzag courses because of the danger from "growlers" — submerged, waterlogged ice floes. Nor did they have their "CAT gear" out. CAT gear was clanking metal pipes, which vessels streamed behind to attract acoustic torpedoes.

On May 6 at 11:40 p.m., "convoy time" — May 7, 12:40 a.m. Newfoundland time — the four corvettes heard an explosion. They thought the *Valleyfield* was dropping practice depth charges, because there were no reports of U-boat activity. The last enemy disposition report had indicated one U-boat 241 kilometres due east and south of Cape Race. It was four minutes before the corvettes realized that the *Valleyfield* had disappeared from Asdic sweeps (anti-submarine detection investigation committee, the British equivalent of sonar).

A torpedo had hit the *Valleyfield* port side, amidships. She broke in half and the forward part sank in less than two minutes. Less than a third of the crew of 12 officers and 152 sailors managed to get over the side in zero-degree (Celsius) water.

Lieutenant Commander Dermott English of St. John's and Boston, the captain, and Lieutenant Tate hit the water together. In civilian life, Dermott English had been captain of the Furness-Withy cruise ship *Monarch* Bermuda. He was not wearing a life jacket. He and Tate clung to a Carley float. Tate remembers the surface was covered with thick bunker "C" oil — "like Vaseline." Three corvettes dropped depth charges. The *Giffard* searched for survivors and picked up 38; 126 were lost.

Tate recalls, "The skipper found a life jacket and slipped it on, but didn't secure it. He looked across the float at me and said, 'Mr. Tate, are you still there? If I don't come out of this alive will you write to my wife?' When the crew of the *Giffard* pulled him out of the water, the only thing they could grab was his life jacket. He slipped out of it, back into the water. We never saw him again."

The survivors were taken to sickbay in St. John's, where they were guinea pigs for a new treatment for hypothermia developed by Dr. Charles Best of insulin fame. Tate says survivors were in the water "from half an hour to an hour and a quarter. The greatest danger was immersion fingers or immersion feet — too cold too long. The accepted treatment was to raise body temperature quickly with warm water. That's when gangrene set in.

"Dr. Best put us all in a room, elevated our feet and hands; fans blew cold air over blocks of ice. We were there 10 days, but it worked. In our group of 38 one man had one finger amputated." New Brunswick Senator Mabel DeWare's brother-in-law, the late Nobel DeWare, was a survivor and later a Moncton fireman. Roy "Buck" Whitlock, a 20-year-old able seaman from Charlottetown, was another survivor. He is better known as one of the Maritimes' finest senior hockey players. He scored 50 or more goals five times with the powerful Moncton, Saint John, and Charlottetown teams. Maritime sportswriters are unanimous in their opinions he was born generations too soon: "In today's NHL he'd be a super star." Halifax broadcaster Pat Connolly, the dean of Maritime sportswriters, says the "time he spent adrift in the cold water was reportedly the cause of leg problems that dogged him throughout his career."

World War II was not just fought "over there." It was fought on Canada's doorstep by a navy whose primary role was convoy escort. All of Britain's oil and most of her war matériel depended on convoys: 26,000 merchant ships crossed the Atlantic carrying 181 million tons.

The east coast war was costly. In 1942, Germany had 300 U-boats, and they hunted in wolf packs of 20. The armed yacht *Raccoon* was torpedoed on September 7, 1942, in the St. Lawrence River. The entire crew of 37 was lost. Four days later, on September 11, 1942, the corvette *Charlottetown* was also torpedoed in the St. Lawrence. A month later, on October 14, 1942, the North Sydney–Newfoundland ferry *Caribou* was torpedoed off Newfoundland; 137 perished. The corvette *Shawinigan* was torpedoed off Cape Breton on November 25, 1944, and 91 crew members were lost. The minesweepers *Clayoquot* and *Esquimalt* were torpedoed near Halifax harbour. The *Esquimalt* went down on April 16, 1945, with a loss of 44 lives — the last Canadian vessel sunk in World War II.

Raymond Goldman, a Glace Bay fish dealer, recalls touring a fish plant in Hamburg in 1967. The manager of the plant was "Herr Koch and he served on a U-boat during the war. He said he developed an ear for cowboy music — especially yodelling — in Canada. He told me 'we used to surface

33

at night off Glace Bay harbour to recharge our batteries and I tuned in to CJCB Radio, Sydney, to listen to Hank Snow, (Hank the Yodelling Ranger), and Wilf Carter.'"

Two Glace Bay fishermen, Joe Young and Jimmy Nolan, were hand lining codfish off Glace Bay when a U-boat surfaced. The conning tower almost capsized them. The submarine crash-dived when a sub-chaser flew overhead. Ian Tate, 82, now lives in Port Hope and has a country retreat near Kinburn. Jake Warren, 80, lives in Chelsea, Quebec, after a distinguished career in the foreign service capped by ambassador's posts in London and Washington.

Chapter 4
Benny Proulx, MBE

I f Benny Proulx hadn't lived, Damon Runyon would have invented him. The kid from Osgoode Street in Ottawa's Sandy Hill district parlayed street smarts and a Lisgar Collegiate education into a storybook career in Asia. Few of his Ottawa friends knew that King George VI awarded him the MBE — Member of the Order of the British Empire — for gallantry in the fall of Hong Kong.

Benny learned to type at Lisgar. When Canadian Pacific advertised for a male stenographer for Japan, he applied. He got the job, moved to Yokohama, and lived in Asia for the next 21 years.

He represented MGM and Paramount Studios in Shanghai, distributing their films in South China, and he had an apartment in Kowloon and a country house several kilo-metres outside the city. A popular member of the Hong Kong Jockey Club, he had a seat on the Hong Kong Stock Exchange and, in 1939, he joined Hong Kong's Royal Naval Volunteers. His wife and two sons enjoyed an *amah* (Asian nanny), cook, maid, gardener, and houseboy. The Proulx family enjoyed the good life — hotel dining and dancing most evenings, and weekends of golf, tennis, and dips in warm Pacific bays. At age 40, Benny had it all. War seemed far away — until the Imperial Japanese forces attacked.

Monday morning, December 8, in Hong Kong was Sunday afternoon, December 7, in Pearl Harbor. Benny, an amateur jockey, was out for a 6 a.m. gallop at Happy Valley racetrack. At 7:30, as a club steward served Benny a breakfast of bacon, eggs, toast, and coffee, he heard air raid sirens, looked up, and saw a V-formation of 15 Japanese bombers. "I could see red balls of the Rising Sun clearly on their wings."

Benny's Royal Navy Volunteers duty post was the Fort Stanley mine-watching station, whose only defence was one 23-centimetre gun. "From my post, I watched helplessly as the Japanese dive-bombed our installations, dropping their eggs with neat precision. Bombs burst among the congested buildings of Hong Kong, vomiting flame and tile, soil and human flesh in brown cones. Then came the order: 'Enemy has landed. Destroy your station. Move to the hills and join the military.'

"In a few minutes we were a roaming band of hillbilly

guerrilla fighters, driving around in search of the enemy. Now that the Japs were in our midst, we could only form small, besieged units, defending each fort, building or hotel in helpless isolation."

Within five days, the Japanese army occupied Hong Kong. Benny joined one of the pockets of resistance in close-quarter fighting. He fought alongside the British Middlesex Regiment before joining the soldiers of Canada's Royal Rifles. He threw hand grenades at attackers. He manned Lewis and Bren guns. When his own .303 rifle went missing, he grabbed a dead Japanese soldier's weapon.

On Christmas Day, Benny sat down to a glum Christmas dinner of "soup, roast chicken, vegetables, tinned peaches with tinned cream and one drink. The dining room rocked as shells whistled through the building and exploded along the upper corridors. For a few moments there, we were gay — not just in our speech — but in our hearts. Briefly, it was Christmas."

At 4:30 p.m., the commanding officer (CO) announced: "The colony has surrendered."

Benny's first thoughts were for his wife and children. "I had a mental image of precisely what would happen when those drug-filled, battle-thirsty Jap soldiers reached our house. Something in me seemed to whisper. Somehow, I reached them by phone and ordered them to drive at once to the Repulse Bay Hotel without stopping for anything. They obeyed to the letter. Shortly afterwards, our front lawn was the scene of a bloody battle, but my family had been saved."

Benny's family carried Irish passports and, because Ireland was neutral, they were allowed safe passage home.

At 6 a.m., Boxing Day, orders came for all British personnel to proceed to the Royal Naval Dockyard. The Japanese Rising Sun flag replaced the Royal Navy Ensign over the dockyard. The entire Hong Kong garrison was interned. Benny's reception was the butt-end of a rifle in his back and, when he fell, another painful blow to his kidneys. His nimble brain stored up all his conquerors' atrocities — bayoneting, beatings, beheadings, and arbitrary executions. He reconstructed the savagery in his best-selling 1943 book, *Underground in Hong Kong*.

In it, he wrote: "We knew well enough that the enemy was not taking prisoners during battle and that anyone surrounded and captured could expect no mercy. They could not even hope for a clean death." Japanese soldiers "were taught to kill ruthlessly and to save ammunition. That is why so many of our soldiers were tied with their hands behind their backs and executed with bayonets instead of bullets." Enemy soldiers "quickly learned to hold life cheaply. Their 'practice' killings are authentically pictured on postcards that can be bought in many parts of the world. The last ones I saw were propped up in a shop window in Capetown. They showed the Japs receiving bayonet practice on live Chinese coolies." On the stone floor of his prison cell, Benny wondered if "my friends made good dummies for Japanese bayonets and I prayed that some of them might still be alive."

During a month of internment, Benny thought only of escape. He discussed the possibility with his "messmates," but found no takers. Two officers of the Royal Netherlands Navy overheard him. They were survivors of a Dutch submarine that had been sunk by Japanese shellfire. The sub sat on the bottom for 30 hours while Japanese destroyers prowled overhead. When the oxygen ran out, the submariners were issued breathing apparatuses and ordered to abandon ship. They followed a rope attached to a surface buoy, stopping several times to decompress. Though in shark-infested waters for 10 hours, oil seeping from the sub kept the predators away. At dawn, Japanese destroyers sighted them and rushed at them, full speed, killing the commander and three crew members.

Benny and the two Dutch submariners made their break for freedom at low tide, midnight, January 27, 1942, making a six-metre drop over a sea wall into soft mud flats covered by 31 centimetres of water. Then, they entered one of Hong Kong's main sewer tunnels and waded through a foul smelling soup of thick sludge and rotting sewage. The first exit they tried was smack dab in the middle of the compound of Japanese army headquarters. The second exit was more successful. Once out, they now had to face climbing Mount Parker, Hong Kong's highest peak.

On the way, they passed a deserted pillbox. Outside the entrance, three Indian soldiers lay dead. Further on, they smelled the sickly odor of six rotting corpses. Two were Indian army soldiers, one a British soldier from the Middlesex regiment, and the three others, Canadians.

All six had been bayoneted.

Benny and his companions scoured the area in search of trenching tools "but we could find no tool or spade with which to dig their graves." There was water everywhere, but none was safe to drink. "Every creek and brook and reservoir was contaminated. You could see dead bodies lying about in the water."

Benny's route to freedom took him to his country home. There, he thought he might find food, water, and money. His house was in darkness. It was empty. Every room had been stripped of furniture. Floors were littered with rubbish, paper, empty tins, decaying food scraps, bloody bandages, and excrement. Japanese soldiers had used every room as a toilet. Even the walls, ceilings, and woodwork were smeared with human waste. There was no food in the house, and the water taps were bone dry. Outside, on the front lawn, were the swollen bodies of several bayoneted Chinese civilians.

Without so much as a backward glance, Benny left his house to rejoin his two Dutch submariner friends. He cast a look along his beach "in the wild hope that there would be a craft anchored off shore. There was none." After two hair-raising days scrambling across the island and several close calls, they managed to negotiate the purchase (with an IOU) of a small boat and oars from a fisherman. Benny's Chinese benefactor was a trusting soul. He accepted a cheque for 300 Hong Kong dollars for a boat and oars.

"A thousand years passed during the next 24 hours. Suspense joined the forces of thirst and hunger and there was no sleep for us … We were able to squeeze a few mouthfuls of drinking water from our wet clothes." All they had to do was row across water patrolled by Japanese gunboats. Their destination was China — "still Jap territory. We'd still have to dodge Japs and walk about 200 miles [322 km] until we'd be among friends. I reached into my breast pocket and took out my crucifix and, holding it in my hand, sat praying like a fool."

The Chinese mainland was five kilometres away. Miraculously, no Japanese patrol boat came near the small craft. No one challenged them. Nine metres from China, their dory hit a submerged rock, splintered, and capsized. They dog-paddled the last few metres to shore. Benny's war wasn't over yet; 59 days after his escape, he reached the headquarters of General Claire Chennault, commanding officer of a group of volunteer U.S. fighter pilots, The Flying Tigers. He served in General Chennault's operations room for two months, until the Tigers were disbanded in July 1942. When the Flying Tigers "stood down," he returned to Canada with hopes of joining Canadian forces. But, at age 40, Benny was "over the hill" — too old for active service. After the war, Benny came home to live in Ottawa.

Retired Ontario Supreme Court Justice Ken Binks remembers him fondly as a likeable character: "When I first met him in the early 1950s, he reminded me of James Cagney, the diminutive movie actor. Benny had the right build for a jockey. At the time, he was selling imported British cars. Shortly after that, at a time when society insisted that you get caught committing (or appear to be committing) adultery in order to obtain a divorce, Benny became a private detective.

"Some thought he took on the airs of Sam Spade, the famous 1930s gumshoe. From time to time, questions were raised about his success rate (some unkind critic said he couldn't have caught anyone in *flagrante delicto* even if he tripped over their bodies at the corner of Bank and Sparks Streets), but he persevered in this calling for a number of years. You could find him any morning at 8:30 in our law office or the parking lot back of the Albion Hotel."

Benny ended his years as a process server, runner, tout, confidential messenger, and confidante to many court-house journalists and prominent members of the criminal bar and judiciary. Ken Binks recalls: "You could always tell when Benny received a new retainer from a suspicious spouse. Immaculately dressed in a blazer, ascot, and beauti-fully pressed grey flannels, (shades of the Hong Kong Jockey Club), he escorted the two senior secretaries from the law offices of Binks and Chilcott out for Friday lunch at Madame Burger's elegant Hull restaurant — to sample the famous *hors d'oeuvres* tray, as he ordered what he described as a dry, very dry 'maw tini.'"

Benny was living on the top floor of an apartment in the Alta Vista neighbourhood (which he irreverently called

"God's Waiting Room") when he died in 1984 at age 83. He spent hours on his balcony observing takeoffs and landings at Uplands Airport with his high-powered field glasses. True to his Hong Kong Jockey Club background, after his death, thousands of discarded lottery tickets were found under his bed. He never did quit trying to pick a winner.

Chapter 5
Tom Fuller

Tom Fuller faced three courts martial and collected a thick file of onion-skin sheets of reprimands. He was also one of Canada's most decorated war heroes. He was awarded the Distinguished Service Cross (DSC) three times and was mentioned in dispatches. A swashbuckling Canadian commander of motor torpedo boats (MTBs) in the pusser (he called it "pukka") British Navy, he didn't just throw the book of MTB warfare away, he re-wrote it his way.

MTBs were fast, wooden, night raiders of the sea that planed on the surface of the water instead of ploughing through it. Constructed with one-centimetre wood topside and double 0.6-centimetre deck planking, but no protective metal cladding, they came in different lengths, ranging from

18 to 36 metres and were capable of speeds of 38 to 47 knots. They carried an assortment of armaments — 46-centimetre or 53-centimetre torpedoes, three-kilogram deck guns, and Lewis and Oerlikons guns. Some were powered by three 1100 hp Rolls-Royce Merlin diesel engines; later models were driven by three 1500 hp Packard gas engines. They were in and out — fast. Tommy's longest fire fight lasted a mere nine and a half minutes.

Tommy was only 30 when the war broke out; his crew, however, called him "Gramps."

Originally, he had tried to join the RCAF. He showed his logbook to numerous recruiting officers. When they realized he was Tom Fuller of Fuller Construction, all they would offer was "Works and Bricks," at best, warrant officer in works and bricks. He finally gave up trying to enlist as a warrior.

Back in Fuller Construction's office in Ottawa's west-end, he received a call from naval officer, O.C.S. "Long Robbie" Robertson, asking if he'd like to join the navy. Fuller thought it was someone from the yacht club pulling his leg. Three days later he was on the *Duchess of Richmond* bound for England.

He needed a uniform run up quickly. The only gold braid available at Preston's military tailor shop was "reserved for Lieutenant Farrow." Preston's phoned Farrow's residence in Hull. His wife answered and said it would be okay, but that Tommy had to drive across Champlain Bridge. She would sew the braid on. And so it was that Hollywood screen star Maureen O'Sullivan became Fuller's seamstress-for-a-day.

Tommy was based on the island of Vis off Yugoslavia, the stronghold of Marshal Tito's guerrillas. Fuller's flotilla of six MTBs sank or captured 24 armed enemy ships in 10 days. He was called "the Pirate of the Adriatic." Superstition holds that cats have nine lives; well, Fuller had 13. That's how many MTBs he had shot out from under him without ever suffering a scratch. He survived 105 fire fights. Fuller won the first of his three Distinguished Service Crosses in the English Channel. He attacked 22 German E-boats (MTBs), anti-aircraft trawlers, and other assorted gunboats. His bold attack so surprised the German armada that, long after he had slipped away in darkness, they were firing away at one another.

Another night in the Bay of Biscay, two U-boats attempted to attack his flotilla. They surfaced simultaneously, collided, and both sank. In another action, he engaged a German destroyer and a squadron of Messerschmitt fighters while warding off three E-boats.

When German paratroopers captured the Greek island of Leros, Tommy was captured and went seven days without sleep. He managed to "liberate" a bottle of rum and shared it with his German guard, who promptly passed out. Tommy then stole an Italian admiral's barge ("We slugged the crew over the head ...") and led an escape group to Turkey. He sold the barge in Turkey for $350, about one-tenth of its value. He was awarded the first bar to his DSC.

Fuller changed the course of torpedo boat warfare. With a deck-load of British commandos, he would ram an enemy vessel. The commandos would board ("… slit a few throats") and seize control of the ship. Fuller would then tow the "prize" back to base. His first prize carried the payroll and Christmas mail for all German troops on the Greek Islands and "a cargo of good Bavarian ale." Subsequent actions netted him boatloads of ammunition, cigarettes, canned goods, firewood, and wheat.

One night, he cut his engines, anchored, and waited. A 400-ton brigantine, bristling with deck guns, sailed by. Her cargo was 10 tons of Danish butter, goulash, and sauerkraut. He towed the ship 84 kilometres to base. At one point, he was 91 metres away from German shore guns, but he was able to slip by unchallenged in darkness. Tommy had been quick to steal German recognition signals. The enemy fired vertical tracer bullets to indicate: "I'm friendly." One of the first things Fuller did was fire a vertical tracer "so we wouldn't get shot at." He entered the harbour at dawn with the German flag flying upside down and prisoners lined up on deck. The Yugoslavs welcomed him with a brass band. Fuller sent three kegs of butter to every Mediterranean flag officer "with the compliments of Tom Fuller." He called it "insurance — in case anyone tried to court martial me for looting."

After one successful capture, Tito presented him with a "complete barrel of the very finest old Proshak wine … it was much appreciated." Tito then honoured him with a dinner.

They dined on Clark's pork and beans ("liberated"), lobster, octopus, and a huge baked fish. As guest of honour, Fuller was given the head and the eyes. During his acts of wartime "piracy," Fuller brought back hundreds of German and Italian prisoners. Most were executed by Tito's guerrillas.

Napoleon said that every corporal had a field marshal's baton in his knapsack. Not Fuller! War was not a career, and promotion was never a priority. He was an acting lieutenant in 1940 and a commander when he was demobbed (demobilized) in 1946, only promoted to captain in 1951. Fuller said that, although he was paid by the Canadian navy, he served in five navies — the Royal Navy (RN), Canadian Navy, American Navy, National Army of Liberation Navy, and the Regia Marina.

His shooting methods were considered unconventional and were dismissed by the British. He was openly critical of one British commander's gunnery tactics and found himself before the captain's mast. He suggested to the captain that they settle the differences in a competition. In force 3 seas, at 30 knots, the British commander's first round landed only 12 metres away. No one could even tell where his second round landed. Fuller adopted a "port attack angle" and fired 457 to 549 metres from the floating target. It disintegrated. A grizzled Royal Navy gunnery NCO who watched said to Fuller: "You know, sir, the Royal Navy travels on 400 years of tradition, but goddamn little efficiency."

Another British officer fell afoul of Fuller's iron will.

He wanted to see action and went along on a night raid. He outranked Fuller and, when the firing started, he panicked, assumed command, and ordered retreat. Fuller hit him over the head with a fire extinguisher, ordered re-engagement, and stood on the unconscious officer during the fire fight.

When the Royal Navy decided it needed a reference book on MTBs, they turned to Fuller. He wrote and dictated a manual and "the RN incorporated practically 100 percent of it." His manual is still the RN's Bible. Tommy had contempt for torpedoes. He once said his torpedo officer "couldn't fire a torpedo and hit the side of a Woolworth building." Leaving England, he had heard there was a shortage of potatoes in the Mediterranean. So, he filled his torpedo tubes with bags of fresh spuds.

He was a consummate scrounger and, at times, a quick thinking thief. He "liberated" sheets of an admiral's personal stationery, which later came in handy when he forged the admiral's signature and ordered American SO radar sets for his flotilla.

"We got everything handed down. The air force didn't like the Vickers engine, so they gave it to us. Hercules engines and Merlin engines and everything [was] handed down from the Royal Air Force. We were the cast-off boys."

He was also inventive. When his "R" mines began exploding prematurely in the water, he wanted to know why. He found that all the plugs under the horns were missing. Spray going over the after deck and humidity was dissolving the plugs. He ordered a midshipman to "go to the base and get a gross of condoms and let's slip condoms over the horns on the mines. The little pink-cheeked Englishman came back without them. He said, 'there's only Wrens in the supply base.'"

"So, I told him I sent him to get condoms, go and bloody well get them. He was pink-cheeked before, he was red-cheeked then, so off he went again.

"I said, 'Did you get them yet?'

"He said, 'Yes, but as I was going out the door, one Wren took a look at the other and said, 'Now, there goes a man!'"

Once, one of his prize trophies was stolen off his bridge. He was billeted at Roedean Ladies' College, Brighton. There was an enameled wall plaque with a hole drilled dead centre to accommodate an electric light switch. The plaque read: *If you feel faint or require the services of a mistress push the button.* He had liberated it and had it installed over his torpedo-firing button.

Tommy was never interested in winning popularity contests with his crew.

"I was the roughest commanding officer of anybody. I would not go on board my ship at night without hailing the Officer of the Watch. When the Officer of the Watch was on deck, I would go down. I figured that if I went down alone with no officer there as a witness, the crew would have thrown me overboard, they hated my guts so much."

When push came to shove, though, his crew stuck with

Tom Fuller (photo courtesy of the Department of National Defence)

him and asked to serve with him if he was transferred. A crew member once told him: "Well, sir, we might be badly damaged, but you always bring us back to port and that's what we want to serve on — a ship that always comes back."

His crews even composed and sang a song for him: "Old Uncle Tom Fuller and His 85-Pound Sledge." Actually, it was an 8.5-pound sledge, but the decimal "got dropped." When he couldn't tow a prize ship back to port, he used the sledge to crack the Kingston valves and scuttle it. He didn't believe in wasting ammunition or explosives when a sledgehammer could do the job.

When the war in Europe ended, he was appointed commanding officer of the HMCS *Naden*, British Columbia. His last rebellious act was on VJ-day — the day Japan surrendered. It was the only time he was ever placed under open arrest. The manager of the local liquor store had closed his outlet. Fuller sent 200 of the toughest looking tattooed sailors he could find in five trucks. Their orders: bring back 25 tons of beer. He told an officer to leave a "chit" and sign his name. When the manager looked outside and saw 200 surly ratings (non-commissioned sailors) swinging their web belts, he had a change of heart. He phoned Fuller's superior, Admiral Brodeur, who told Fuller to consider himself under open arrest. Fuller told the admiral he didn't steal the beverage.

"I signed for it," he boldly declared.

In later years, Tommy delighted in mimicking Admiral Brodeur's broken English: "consider yourself hunder hopen harrest. Be hin my office at ho-height-double-ho in the morning by the first haircraft."

He left behind a rich and ribald 42-page oral history in volume one of *Salty Bits*, the nine-volume collection of individual war stories published by the Naval Officers' Association. Fuller recounted how he was ousted from the ex-German ambassador's residence on the Island of Ischia, near Capri. The villa was required for two VIPs, who turned out to be Winston Churchill and King George VI.

"Churchill, with a great big straw hat, towel over his arm, naked as the day he was born, went down the path to the highway, stopped the traffic this way, stopped the traffic that way, and walked across. Not the towel around him, just over his arm. He went down and plunged into the harbour and then he dried himself with the towel and walked up. Stopped the traffic this way and stopped the traffic that way, with George saying: 'Churchill, put some clothes on!'"

Tommy Fuller died in May 1994. He was 85. His coffin was placed on a gun carriage pulled by naval pallbearers to Christ Church Cathedral. His double-mast brigantine, *Black Jack*, boomed out a seven-gun salute. En route to Beechwood Cemetery, the cortege stopped twice. A piper played "Amazing Grace" in front of the Parliament buildings his grandfather built. The second stop was at the War Museum, where the flag was lowered.

Tommy Fuller served longer than any other man in attack warfare. He was 10 years older than anyone else on the job.

Chapter 6
Grounded in China

I n 1954, RCAF Squadron Leader Andy MacKenzie sat down to enjoy a traditional Christmas dinner with his wife and four children in the family's new home in Strathmore, near Pointe Claire, on the island of Montreal. Andy's father carved the turkey. The previous two Christmases, he had eaten rice and steamed bread in solitary confinement in Chinese and North Korean prisoner-of-war camps.

Andy was one of 22 Canadian exchange pilots serving with the 51st Wing, U.S. 5th Air Force. He was the only Canadian pilot shot down in Korea and taken prisoner. His Sabre was destroyed by "friendly" cannon fire from a U.S. captain.

"My canopy was blown off. My right aileron [hinged

surface in the trailing edge of the wing used to control roll about the longitudinal axis] was hit, and my instrument panel was destroyed. My aircraft was out of control. I was starting to roll to the left. I was barrelling towards the ground. I could see Russian MiG fire chasing me like little hot tennis balls. There was no point staying with the plane, so I punched out." Floating down, he could see the Yalu River, a power station, part of northeast China, and the mountains of North Korea.

"I was over North Korea, 10 miles [16 km] south of the Yalu River."

He could also see two trucks full of soldiers heading in his direction. His original plan was to discard his gear, head for the mountains, and "with luck I might hide and wait for nightfall." There were 30 soldiers, some armed with Tommy guns, hard on his heels. They fired warning shots, and bullets pinged off rocks around him. He had no choice but to stand, face his pursuers, and surrender. They made no attempt to harm him. They motioned him to put his hands up and stripped him of his .45 calibre sidearm, G-suit, Mae West life-jacket, cigarettes, and lighter. Andy recalls that the majority of the soldiers were Chinese, but "I noticed one North Korean officer. The leader of the group was Chinese." He was blindfolded, thrown into the back of a truck, and driven across the Yalu River into China.

For two years he was a prisoner, spending 18 months in solitary confinement after two failed escape attempts. He got about 90 centimetres from the main gate, where he ran into guards with fixed bayonets in the dark. "For punishment," he says, "they took away my wooden bed and left me with only a mattress of woven straw and a blanket."

He subsisted on a diet of rice and steamed bread. At capture, he weighed 195 pounds. By the time he was released, his weight had dropped to 120 pounds.

"I didn't eat raw vegetables, because farmers fertilized their crops with human excrement and I didn't want to risk diseases. I had no idea what was going to happen to me. Every time I was handcuffed, blindfolded, and thrown into the back of a vehicle, I thought they were taking me to the killing ground. I believed that no prisoners of war had ever returned from a genuine Chinese prisoner-of-war camp. I believed that the Chinese didn't take prisoners."

"One day, another prisoner, a B-29 tail-gunner, peered through the gaps in my log house and saw my blue eyes. I passed him a note saying who I was and asked him to get it to my wife."

Eighteen months after his capture, his wife, Joyce, had proof Andy was alive. At this point, the Canadian government stepped in. Chester Ronning was the foremost Far East expert in the West. Fluent in Mandarin, he was the senior Canadian diplomat in China when the People's Republic was declared in 1949. He represented Canada at the conference that negotiated the Korean cease-fire, where he began a friendship with Chinese Premier Chou En-lai.

Ottawa sent Ronning to a 1954 conference in China with instructions to ask Chou En-lai if the Chinese were keeping Andy MacKenzie prisoner. Ronning made his case with the Chinese premier and added: "He has a wife and four children." Chou En-lai promised MacKenzie's release and six months later Andy was freed. It was almost 17 months after the July 27, 1953, cease-fire.

Because of Joyce's persistence, the RCAF didn't close Andy's file. His original casualty record read: "Lost while on combat mission over NK. S/L MacKenzie was last seen at XE 4767 (6135-111) near Uji, North Korea." It was later amended: "POW/Repatriated." Joyce had convinced them he was alive.

Andy says: "I was shot down at 1 p.m. on December 4, 1952, and released two years later to the minute — 1 p.m., on December 4, 1954. I think I may have been tried in absentia and sentenced to two years, but I was never in a court. Three U.S. pilots, Captain Hal Fisher and Lieutenants Lyle Cameron and Ron Parks were all tried and given two years. Hal Fisher ended up as a colonel and lives in Vegas. Lyle Cameron wound up as a four-star general and lives in Dallas. Ron Parks lives in Omaha. We keep in touch." Andy MacKenzie had no desire to "keep in touch" with the wingman who shot him down.

Years later, in Torbay, Newfoundland, U.S. Major General Barcus gave him an unofficial apology, saying the U.S. pilot was "remorseful" and had "asked to be taken off operations." He was assigned to ferrying fighter jets to Japan for maintenance and was killed when he flew into a mountain in a bad-weather approach.

The day of his release, Andy was driven 177 kilometres to Canton from Mukden, near Shenyang. The Chinese would not release him until he signed three pages of foolscap written in "a fine hand in India ink. The language was precise and grammatically perfect. The 'confession' was false. I was shot down 10 miles [16 km] inside North Korea — not China. They wanted me to agree I had been shot down over China, that I was spying for the U.S., and that I was taken prisoner in China. I signed the false statement and I have no idea where it ended up.

"They drove me to a bridge and indicated I was free and should cross. They asked me to wave goodbye to a guy who was operating an 8 mm movie camera on a hillside. I took off across that 150-yard [137-m] bridge at 180 miles [290 km] an hour. I was wearing traditional Chinese garb."

His first meal in Kowloon was a "big thick steak." Examined by doctors for three or four days, he was then flown to Tokyo. The RCAF flew him to Sea Island, British Columbia, where his wife and children awaited. Andy had 90 days leave coming.

Ottawa rolled out the red carpet. Prime Minister Louis St. Laurent received him, as did External Affairs Minister Lester B. Pearson. St. Laurent, says Andy, "did a very warm thing. He came out from behind his desk, dragged a chair to the front of his desk and we sat knee-to-knee."

Defence Minister Ralph Campney was less than hospitable. Campney looked at him and said: "Sorry I don't have a bowl of rice for you, Andy." Pearson, who had taken Andy under his wing and brought him to see Campney, immediately rebuked the minister for his sick humour.

Andy went back to duty as an instructor at Chatham. Then he was posted to Kansas City, Missouri, to serve with the 29th North American Air Defence Command (NORAD) Region. He finished his career as chief administrative officer at Rockcliffe.

Before the Korean conflict, Andy had been a World War II fighter ace. He was credited with destroying eight-and-a-half Luftwaffe planes — three of them in only 90 seconds. He was shot down twice by anti-aircraft fire, once by U.S. gunners over Utah Beach in Normandy. The second time, he was hit by enemy flak at 18,000 feet and made a dead-stick landing behind his lines. He accumulated 800 hours in fighters and flew 157 missions. His fifth mission in Korea was his last. After serving 26 years in the RCAF, he retired in 1966 to a stone house with 100 acres in Oxford Station, south of Ottawa.

Twenty-four years later, Andy returned to Korea with a Canadian delegation to observe the 25th anniversary of the Korean War.

Chapter 7
Caribou Torpedoed

On October 13, 1942, the Cape Breton–Newfoundland ferry, SS *Caribou*, slipped her moorings for a regular overnight run from North Sydney to Port aux Basques. The *Caribou* made smoke at 9:45 p.m. on a clear, calm, starlit night. Six hours later, she was on the bottom in 250 fathoms just off St. Paul's Island, two hours out of Port aux Basques, Newfoundland.

The *Caribou* took one torpedo amidships from U-boat U-69 and sank almost perpendicularly in three minutes. The torpedo went straight through, exiting on the opposite side. She carried 192 passengers and a crew of 47. Her manifest included 119 Canadian, U.S., and British servicemen and 73 civilians; 104 passengers and 31 crew members died. There were 101 survivors.

Caribou *Torpedoed*

The captain, Benjamin Tavernor, and two of his sons, First Mate Harold and Third Officer Stanley, went down with the ship. The Tapper family of Grand Beach, Newfoundland, lost five sons who were crew members.

Jane's Fighting Ships records a lean obituary:

CARIBOU (1925), 2,222 tons gross, Newfoundland Government Service. Torpedoed by enemy submarine in Cabot Strait, October 14, 1942.

Eyewitness reports from the Canadian navy escort, HMCS *Grandmere*, stated that Captain Tavernor attempted to ram the U-boat, but there was little likelihood his ship could have covered the 1,372 metres before she slipped under the waves. Kapitanleutnant Ulrich Graf fired one torpedo that sliced completely through the *Caribou*. German naval archives recorded that the weather was fair, visibility was very good, wind was two, and motion of the sea, one.

U-69's logbook records:

Result 1 hit/attack shot. Torpedo depth was set at 10 feet [3 m], firing angle 200.5 degrees, course 333.9 degrees and running time 43 seconds.

... high, dark burst with red-glowing parts. Shortly afterwards second explosion (boiler). Steamer immediately sinks as far as guardrail, lists towards (illegible) ... long-lasting breaking of bulk-

heads can be heard everywhere in the submarine. Comment, opinion and decision: hit, attack shot.

Rumours that U-69 remained on the surface and machine-gunned survivors are just that — rumours. There was not enough time. U-69, nicknamed "Laughing Cow" by her crew, was taking evasive action to slip away.

The *Grandmere*, a Bangor class minesweeper, was only 1,372 metres off the *Caribou*'s starboard bow. She altered course to ram, but the U-boat dived when she was still 137 metres away. The *Grandmere* dropped six depth charges set for 150 feet (46 m) and then two more set for 500 feet (152 m). A later naval inquiry queried the *Grandmere*'s strategy because, given time and distance, the U-69 could only have travelled 91 metres and reached a depth of 75 feet (23 m). U-69 slipped away to fight another day. Four months later, the HMS *Viscount* sank her in the Atlantic.

Strict Canadian censorship kept the news from the public for three days, but the English traitor, William Joyce, broadcasting as Lord Haw Haw, trumpeted the sinking the same day. Lord Haw Haw's propaganda radio broadcasts were daytime transmissions that only local residents with powerful Hallicrafter receivers could pick up. Maritime homes with normal radios could sometimes receive short wave transmissions from Europe on cold, crisp winter nights.

Jack O'Brien from Amherst, Nova Scotia, was a 19-year-old AC1 in the RCAF. His mother heard Lord Haw Haw on the radio, but she thought Jack was on the *Lady Rodney* bearing for Halifax.

"Her doorbell rang," Jack says, "and it was a telegram from Ottawa saying I was rescued at an Eastern Canadian port and she was not to divulge the information and it was signed by the RCAF Casualty Office." Jack recalls hearing "the screaming of women and children who went down. Lucky for me I went swimming in an old stone quarry! The water wasn't a bit colder than the spring-fed swimming hole."

O'Brien shared a cabin with four non-commissioned airmen from Prince Edward Island. He was asleep in a top bunk and ended up on the deck when the torpedo struck. He grabbed his pants and greatcoat and was met by a flood of water rushing down a companionway. He never saw his four cabin mates again. He put a life belt on, but saw a woman at the rail without one. He put his belt on her and pushed her over the side. She survived. He swam towards a piece of floating wreckage and away from the ship's suction. He was blown off his makeshift raft when the *Grandmere*'s depth charges threw up geysers of water.

The *Caribou* carried lifeboats for 300. O'Brien clambered into one and shared it with 19 others for five hours in water up to their waists. Another survivor, Gerald Bastow, speaking to a St. John's Rotary Club, said he could never understand how Jack O'Brien managed to survive in the water in his heavy air force greatcoat but "there he was, sitting on a raft, with a small infant tucked away inside the coat on both sides of his chest."

They kept their spirits up by singing, and "when daylight came, a navy vessel which had been steaming around dropping depth charges was able to pick us up."

Charlie Moores of St. John's said the only thing he saved was his watch, which "incidentally, kept going all night." He recalls going ashore in Sydney with his shoes "still unlaced." He remembers seeing one survivor climbing a rope ladder lowered by the *Grandmere*. He was "clad only in his long johns, but he had his wallet clenched firmly in his teeth."

Nursing Sister Agnes Wightman Wilkie from Carmen, Manitoba, was the first and only woman serving in the Canadian navy to lose her life as a result of enemy action. She was only 30 years old. Her companion, nursing dietician Margaret Martha Brooke of Ardath, Saskatchewan, attempted in vain to save her life and was decorated for gallantry and courage. She was awarded an MBE. Petty Officer John Barrett and his bride of two weeks were going home to Curling to visit his parents. Mrs. Barrett was rescued, but Petty Officer Barrett perished.

"Baby P," an unidentified and unclaimed blond baby boy died after being taken aboard the *Grandmere*. The only means of identification was a tiny signet ring bearing the initial "P." The city of Sydney buried "Baby P" and a naval honour guard from HMCS Dockyard marched in the funeral procession.

Navy minister, Angus L. Macdonald, told Canada's House of Commons that the torpedoing "brings the war to

Canada with tragic emphasis ... if there were any Canadians who did not realize that we are up against a ruthless and remorseless enemy there can be no such Canadians now."

Was the *Caribou* fair game because it was a quasi-troop ship? Why did the Canadian navy insist on night crossings when ships' captains and the Newfoundland Marine Railway were opposed? Why were sailings on regular schedules at fixed times? Why did the *Grandmere* set her depth charges to explode too deep at 150 (46 m) and 500 feet (152 m)?

The wolf pack roamed from Newfoundland to the Panama Canal and, along the Atlantic seaboard, Nazi subs sent two and a half million tons of Allied shipping to the bottom in six months. By the summer of 1942, U-boats were sinking a ship every four hours. The *Caribou* was the last victim of the Battle of the Atlantic.

After the *Caribou* went down, the U-boats put out to sea. The *Caribou* was remembered on a Canadian postage stamp, and posters asked Canadians in Atlantic Canada to "Remember the *Caribou*." At the foot of Lookout Hill, Port aux Basques, is an eight-metre high marble cenotaph topped by a bronze caribou. An amber light burns in perpetuity. Attached to the marble plinth are bronze plaques with the names of those who died.

Chapter 8
German P.O.W. Camps in Canada

T he last prisoner of war (P.O.W.) camp in
Canada in Monteith, Ontario, northeast of
Timmins, closed 60 years ago. The last of
35,046 P.O.W.'s went home. They were interned in 26 maximum-security enclosures and scores of small minimum-
security work camps scattered across Canada.

Camp 20, Gravenhurst ("Muskoka Officers' Camp")
housed 400 officers in a converted sanatorium. Bowmanville
("Lake Ontario Officers' Camp") caged 750 officers in a boys'
reformatory. Espanola's camp was a factory, Lethbridge's a
collection of barracks, Kingston's a fort, and Hull's an abandoned jail where Canadian communists were imprisoned.

Camp 43, Ile Ste. Helene, Montreal, was the smallest
maximum-security camp. The millions who visited the Expo

'67 island were probably unaware that 300 German prisoners had sat out their war there. The largest camp, 12,500 prisoners, was in Lethbridge.

The first camps opened in Petawawa and Kananaskis, near Calgary, in September 1939. They were not military compounds exclusively. Aliens in Britain when war broke out were interned. Canadian citizens and landed immigrants considered security risks were detained. Aliens on ships docked in Canadian ports wound up behind barbed wire.

Eight hundred civilians were locked up separately from military prisoners. The highest profile civilian was Montreal Mayor Camilien Houde. He exhorted Quebecois to boycott conscription. He was interned in Petawawa for four years (1940–1944), without being charged or tried. The flamboyant politician was a Francophone twin of colourful New York Mayor, Fiorello LaGuardia. After his release, Houde was re-elected mayor and member of the assembly. In 1949, at Toronto's Varsity Stadium, he kicked off the ceremonial ball when Montreal defeated Calgary 28-15 to win its first Grey Cup. When officials thanked him, the impish chief magistrate told English Canada he would be happy to come back every year and "kick all your balls off."

Canadian communists, fascists, militant union bosses, and conscription opponents were rounded up; 130 Canadians "believed to be communists" were arbitrarily interned. Prominent Quebec fascist, Adrien Arcand, was jailed. Seaman's Union president, Pat Sullivan, Nova Scotia fishermen's union chief, Charles Murray, electrical workers union president, C. S. Jackson, and Windsor United Auto Workers' organizer, Bill Walsh, were incarcerated.

Walsh was detained from 1940 to 1942 and released. He was forbidden to leave Windsor and was required to report to the Royal Canadian Mounted Police (RCMP). He violated both conditions. The RCMP went looking for him. The trail led to France. A Mountie waited to interview the intelligence officer of a Canadian battalion preparing to assault the Siegfreid Line. He didn't know the intelligence officer was Bill Walsh. Communist Party leaders Tim Buck, Sam Carr, and Charles Sims fled to the United States to avoid detention.

A little known chapter in Canada's war was the involvement of Canadian communists. At the request of Britain's Strategic Operations Executive (SOE) and the U.S. Office of Strategic Services (OSS), the RCMP, the Canadian Communist Party, and the Departments of Defence and External Affairs combined to create a secret commando unit. The Communist Party provided lists of Canadian communists of Yugoslav, Bulgarian, and Hungarian descent. Sixty volunteers were recruited, trained in Canada, Palestine, and Egypt, and parachuted behind enemy lines into Yugoslavia and the Balkans. Their mission was to link up with resistance fighters, sabotage enemy assets, gather intelligence, and harass enemy forces.

Meanwhile, converted liners — the *Queen Mary*, the *Ile de France*, and the *Duchess of York* — transported Allied troops to Britain, deadheading back to Canada with P.O.W.'s for internment. In July 1940, U-boat U-47 torpedoed the British liner, *Arandora Star,* 161 kilometres west of Ireland. Half the 1,600 German P.O.W.'s on board perished.

Liners docked in Halifax or Quebec, and trains took prisoners to camps. Each coach carried three guards armed only with whistles and small leather blackjacks. The guards belonged to the Department of National Defence's Veterans Guard. By June 1943, there were 11,000 Veterans Guards. Their maximum age was 50.

Over five years, the Guards lost only one prisoner. Luftwaffe ace, Franz von Werra ("The One That Got Away"), jumped from a train into a snowbank in Smiths Falls and made a "home run" to Germany. He used his hands as paddles to guide a stolen rowboat across the slush covered St. Lawrence River to neutral territory in the United States. Germany's consul in New York secretly delivered him home to Germany through Mexico and South America. He was given a tumultuous hero's welcome in Berlin and decorated personally by Deputy Fuhrer Hermann Goring. The swashbuckling von Werra claimed he was a baron and was photographed alongside his fighter with his pet lion cub. He was killed when the engine of his ME109 seized and he crashed in the North Sea.

Canada's internment operations bureaucracy operated out of Rooms 283, 285, and 285A of the West Block of Parliament. The director was Brigadier General Edouard de Panet, a World War I veteran of the First Canadian Division.

His deputy was Lieutenant Colonel Hubert Stetham, Royal Military College faculty member and Kingston city councillor.

Prisoners were treated well. Some were contracted out as day labourers on farms. They were paid 50 cents a day. Some, in remote bush locations, were trusted with rifles and allowed to hunt game. Food allotments were comparable to civilian portions — equivalent quantities of rationed items — butter, sugar, tea, coffee, eggs, meat, fish, jam, fresh fruit, and vegetables. When their uniforms wore out, P.O.W.'s were given replacement clothing, dark blue trousers with a red stripe across the right leg and shirts and tunics with red circles painted on the backs.

Every camp had a working still. Copper piping was liberated from camp plumbing, while sugar and raisins were stolen from kitchens. Bowmanville had a large contingent of thirsty Afrika Korps desert troops. A friendly guard became friendlier when he took a shine to their "shine" and provided all the copper tubing they needed.

In Espanola, a mahogany piano vanished. Prisoners shaved the hardwood upright, mixed it with tobacco, and smoked it. Guards routinely inspected pianos for prisoners hiding inside. Before a coffin was carried to a graveyard outside camp, guards opened it to catch any escapee piggybacking out on top of the deceased. Espanola P.O.W.'s pursued a profitable sideline casting fake Iron Crosses and selling them to unsuspecting guards. In Farnham, Quebec, an air show promoter paid three German paratroopers $10 each to jump.

They spent the money on liquor and were blind drunk when they jumped. No camp was without a homemade radio. Kingston prisoners concealed theirs in waterproof wrapping in the roots of a potted plant.

Homosexual activity was rare, but not unknown. Punishment for homosexual acts was administered by peers and was swift. At Monteith, a prisoner who propositioned a sailor ended up with a battered face, two black eyes, and 28 days in detention.

Kingston prisoners revolted when black soldiers were assigned to guard them. They informed the camp commandant in a written protest that "coloured people" were not acceptable. Lake Superior P.O.W.'s complained that a camp hospital doctor was Jewish.

Escape attempts were frequent and unsuccessful. Two P.O.W.'s escaped from Kingston and crossed the St. Lawrence to Clayton, New York. The United States sent them back. Nineteen Kingston P.O.W.'s escaped by tunnelling under a stone wall. All were captured. Camp X in Angler, 400 kilometres northwest of Sault Ste. Marie and 150 kilometres from the U.S. border held 560 P.O.W.'s. Twenty-eight broke out in April 1941: two were shot dead and three were wounded. Two got away, but were free only briefly.

One escapee was 2,000 kilometres from Angler when the FBI nabbed him. He crossed the river to Detroit from Windsor and reached Texas. A Detroit Nazi sympathizer who helped him was convicted of treason and sentenced to hang. Twenty-four hours before his scheduled execution, President Roosevelt commuted his sentence. The globetrotting escapee was returned to Angler and given 28 days in detention.

In April 1942, two Luftwaffe officers escaped from Bowmanville and were picked up in Niagara Falls the next day.

Five thousand hard-core Nazis were imprisoned in Camp 132, Medicine Hat. On two separate occasions, SS troops accused a prisoner of being communist and anti-Nazi. Ringleaders presided over kangaroo courts. The accused men were found guilty and lynched. In July 1943, a court found three prisoners guilty of the first murder. One was hanged. In December 1946, four P.O.W.'s were convicted of the second murder and hanged.

The Veterans' Guard made it abundantly clear that media attention was unwelcome. *Toronto Star* reporter Doug MacFarlane was arrested when he stepped down from a train near a camp. *Toronto Telegram* reporter Scott Young had his notes confiscated and burned.

On V-E Day, all hell broke loose in Gravenhurst. There was cheering; horns blew, and ecstatic citizens danced in the streets. A prisoner asked a guard what the uproar was about. The guard responded: "The war is over." The P.O.W.'s rejoinder: "Who won?"

When hostilities ended, many P.O.W.'s wanted to stay in Canada, but the Geneva Convention stipulated repatriation to Germany. Many came back, married Canadian girls, and established businesses near the camps where they were imprisoned.

On a Danube cruise from Vienna to the Black Sea, Janet and I were assigned a dining table. Our companions for 10 days were a retired oil company executive and his wife. He spent most of his war as a P.O.W. in the Muskokas. He told us he escaped once and avoided detection by hiding under water in eel grass in Pine Lake. He breathed through a hollow reed. The only clothing he wore was a bathing suit. He said the mosquitoes and black flies were so thick he gave himself up, happy to return to the relative cold comfort of barbed wire.

Chapter 9
Jack Munroe
and Bobbie Burns

John Alexander "Jack" Munroe was one of the most extraordinary and least known Canadians who ever lived.

He was born on a farm at Upper Kempt Head, 18 kilometres from Boularderie, Cape Breton, in 1873. He was a prospector, a hard-running star halfback on a championship football team in the highly competitive western United States high school conference, a five-year professional star in football-mad Montana, a professional boxer and wrestler, a World War I hero, a poet, a gifted author, and the reeve of boomtown Elk Lake in northern Ontario. He defeated the heavyweight champion of the world in a four-round bout in Butte, Montana, in 1902. In Ontario's North, he is still remembered as the man who organized the fire brigade that saved Elk Lake in the great Porcupine Forest fire of 1911.

He may have been the very first Canadian soldier to set foot on French soil in World War I. Before the ship's gangplank could be fully deployed, Munroe jumped from the deck onto French soil.

When he was 12 years old, he left Cape Breton with two of his brothers to seek their fortunes in Nevada and Montana. Butte was one of the toughest and most lawless mining towns in North America. Standard dress accessories were a pair of Colt revolvers and a Bowie knife. Even feared peacekeepers Bat Masterson and Wyatt Earp gave Butte a miss.

On December 20, 1902, Munroe defeated world heavyweight boxing champion, James J. Jeffries, in a four-round bout in Butte. Munroe gave as good as he took for three rounds and then decked the champion for a count of nine in the fourth round. His purse was $250.

In February 1904, he gave top ranked heavyweight contender Tom Sharkey a fierce beating in a six-round bout in Philadelphia. Sharkey was still on his feet at the end of the fight, but both his eyes were closed. Munroe didn't have a mark on him. In November 1904, Munroe knocked out Peter Maher, heavyweight champion of Ireland, in the fourth round in Philadelphia. Munroe had 20 major fights and won nine by knockouts. He lost only three fights. His last fight was in April 1906, in Lavigne's Hall in Hull. He knocked out Ottawa's Alf Allen in the eighth round. Munroe squirrelled away his wages and fight purses to invest in prospecting for base metals and precious metals.

In Mexico City, a fully-grown stray male collie dog adopted him. They bonded immediately and Jack Munroe and "Bobbie Burns" became inseparable. Jack told his friends that in another incarnation Bobbie Burns was Highland royalty. Bobbie was with Jack when he presented himself at Lansdowne Park, Ottawa, to enlist in the newly formed Princess Patricia's Canadian Light Infantry (PPCLI). The unit was named after Princess Patricia, daughter of Canada's Governor General, the Duke of Connaught, Queen Victoria's youngest son.

The Pats were formed in August 1914, after wealthy Montreal businessman, Hamilton Gault, pledged $100,000 for a volunteer infantry battalion. The regiment had the best equipment: Lee Enfield rifles, instead of the unreliable Ross rifles, and Penetanguishene boots, instead of the shoddy footwear issued to other Canadian troops. Bobbie Burns enlisted, too. Princess Patricia proclaimed him regimental mascot of the PPCLI. She presented him with an expensive jewelled collar inscribed: BOBBIE BURNS. PPCLI.

While the regiment was bivouacked at Levis, Quebec, awaiting passage to England, Bobbie was kidnapped. Frantic Pats fanned out and searched the countryside. He was found a week later, tied up, at Valcartier. He had refused all food and drink during his captivity.

Bobbie went everywhere with Jack. He was smuggled on board trains, carried onto a troop ship in a gunny sack, and slipped past England's animal quarantine inspectors. He also followed Jack to the Western Front in the second battle for Ypres. Bobbie Burns was treated as a minor god from the colonel on down.

When the PPCLI crossed the English Channel to France they were 1,000 strong. The regiment was reinforced with drafts of 800 men. When the battle for Ypres was over, there were only 133 left. Munroe's regiment fought off the Germans under the most appalling conditions — trench warfare, mud, rats, lice, the stench of decaying human and animal flesh, constant artillery barrages, German snipers with newfangled telescopic sights that enabled them to pick off a man 1,829 metres away, a shortage of food and ammunition, and two and three days on end without sleep.

Jack told his mining buddies that Bobbie Burns went out with him on "recce" missions. He said that even though Bobbie was a collie, he had all the instincts of a pointer. When he spotted an enemy soldier across no-man's land, his body would go rigid and his tail stood straight out.

The Pats stopped the German advance in a heroic but costly stand at Pollegon Wood and carried the day. If the Germans had broken through, they would have taken Ypres and bullied their way through to Calais. Jack led a platoon that captured 90 German prisoners. He wasn't awarded any major gongs for bravery in the living hell that was Ypres. Yet, he earned the highest award possible: he survived.

On June 16, 1916, Jack was shot in the right chest by a sniper near Armentieres. The bullet exited very close to his spinal column. Arterial blood spurted out until one of Jack's comrades stuck his finger in the bullet hole and staunched the flow. The medical officer told Jack his life depended on remaining perfectly still, lest he bleed to death. Four days later he was invalided to Royal Victoria Hospital in Netley, 113 kilometres from London. The hospital commandant issued an order that Bobbie Burns be permitted to stay at Jack's bedside and have the run of the hospital. Despite further surgeries, Jack's strong right arm would hang useless at his side for the rest of his life.

Queen Mother Alexandra, the widow of King Edward VII, visited the wounded soldiers in hospital. Jack noted later in his mini-classic book, *Mopping Up*, that the Queen Mother met Bobbie and had some "kind words" for him. "Bobbie was pleased," Jack noted. The dog liked attention, but he was not overwhelmed. *Mopping Up* was a book Jack wrote in 1918. It was a stark, sensitive, and extremely well written first person story told through Bobbie's eyes.

After the war, Jack was prospecting unsuccessfully in a remote region near Hurst. He caught a train "at a lonely station" and took it for granted that Bobbie was under his seat. But Bobbie missed the train, and Jack believed he had seen the last of his beloved companion.

The train carried Jack to Porcupine. Ten days later, "Bobbie trotted into Porcupine." He had covered 322 kilometres of "as rough, unbroken country as there is in the world." Bobbie was "somewhat thin and not a little weary" but he "upreared and flung his forepaws upon my shoulders, the happiest, wriggling, home-coming prodigal son of a collie in Canada, or in all the world."

Jack and Bobbie came home to Canada to dull desk jobs in recruiting offices. Jack was commissioned a lieutenant and given permission to join the Liberty Bond speaking tour in the United States, where he was a popular drawing card. He was discharged in December 1918.

Jack and Bobbie went to Nova Scotia to visit his ailing mother and family. Their next stop was northern Ontario, to claim his fortune in goal and silver mines. Jack got extremely rich selling claims, but he hadn't fallen off a turnip truck from Boularderie. He kept a small percentage interest in each claim. He parlayed his riches into hotels and commercial realty in Ontario's northland. In 1923, at the age of 50, Jack married Lina, a Toronto concert soprano, who was 10 years younger. He died on February 12, 1942, at the age of 69. He is buried in his wife's family plot in Acton.

Bobbie Burns was 16 years old when he died in 1919. One day he simply failed to meet Jack's train at the station. He had crawled off into the woods to die. Munroe refused to search for Bobbie. He reasoned that Bobbie knew his time had come and he chose not to disturb his final resting place. Jack mourned for Bobbie Burns and could never bring himself to replace him with another pet.

Immortalized in *The Ballad of Jack Munroe*, an anonymous piece of war poetry published in 1918, Jack Munroe was inducted in the Canadian Boxing Hall of Fame; he is an Original Member of Nova Scotia's Sport Hall of Fame.

Chapter 10
The Fuhrer's Yacht

After World War II, Bob Rodney of Ottawa was a teenage dropout from Westboro's Churchill Public School on his first visit to New York. Hitler's yacht was pointed out to him in the Brooklyn Navy Yards. He literally shot from the hip when he photographed the 86-foot wooden tall ship with a cheap plastic Brownie camera. The navy shore patrol was hard on his heels. "Military brass were not anxious for the public to see the yacht they 'liberated' and generals used as their plaything."

Adolf Hitler's yacht, the *Ostwind*, went to join the Valkyries in 42 fathoms of water off Miami 44 years after the war ended. At least, that's what the game plan called for. But Hitler must have enjoyed the last laugh. Because of human error and rough one-metre seas, the clapped-out hull was dropped off a barge onto a six-metre high healthy reef of coral and sponges in only six fathoms of water.

Miami Commissioner Abe Resnick, a Holocaust survivor from Lithuania, had organized the event to mark the 50th anniversary of the June 5, 1939, "voyage of the damned." A plane flew overhead trailing a banner that read: "NEVER AGAIN."

The *Voyage of the Damned* was the saga of the passenger ship *St. Louis*, which sailed from Hamburg on May 15, 1939, with 907 German Jews on board. The entire ship's complement had been given Cuban entrance visas before leaving Hamburg, but when the *St. Louis* docked in Havana, her passengers learned that their visas had been revoked. One after another, South American nations Argentina, Uruguay, Paraguay, and Panama denied them entry. The United States not only refused them entry, but also sent a Coast Guard cutter to ensure the captain did not run the ship aground to allow refugees to swim ashore. Canada's King government also turned the *St. Louis* away.

Canada's Immigration Branch was a minor agency attached to the Ministry of Mines and Resources. The minister, Tom Crerar, was a 32-year Commons veteran awaiting a summons to the Senate. He left the day-to-day responsibility for immigration to a public servant, Frederick Charles Blair. Blair was a one-man band. He considered immigration his personal fiefdom. Blair's anti-Semitism was in the open.

He was on the record stating the term "refugee" was a code word for Jew and warned his minister that, unless safeguards were adopted, Canada was in danger of being "flooded with Jewish people." Crerar relied totally on Blair, whose personal immigration policy was that immigrants should be kept out. Referring to Jewish immigrants, Blair wrote in a letter: "None is too many." The phrase later became the title of a best-selling book by Toronto university professor, Irving Abella.

Blair had an ally in nationally known social worker and future mayor of Ottawa Charlotte Whitton. Dr. Whitton repeatedly admonished members of the National Refugee Committee to focus on non-Jewish refugees. She sent a memo to all welfare councils warning of large numbers of non-British refugee children.

Oscar Cohen, prominent Jewish activist, almost broke up the inaugural meeting of the National Refugee Committee when he charged that Charlotte Whitton was carrying on "guerrilla warfare against the Canadian Jewish Council by trying to block the refugee children project."

Charlotte Whitton was not alone in adopting an anti-Jewish stance. Mackenzie King's Liberal government turned *laissez-faire* blind eyes and deaf ears to Frederick Blair's blatant discrimination. In 1926, King purchased Shady Hill cottage and a lot of land at Kingsmere for $1,400. His diary entry recorded the only reason he bought the property was to prevent "a sale to Jews who have a desire to get in at Kingsmere & would ruin the whole place."

The *St. Louis* had no alternative but to return to Hamburg with its human cargo. Half of the 907 Jews died in the gas chambers and crematoria of Nazi death camps. Twenty-six surviving members of the *St. Louis* were on hand to watch the *Ostwind* being scuttled. Rabbi Barry Konovitch told the 300 assembled, including 60 journalists from around the world: "it will become an artificial reef. It's nice to think that some good will come of it — at last."

Describing the *Ostwind* as "Hitler's yacht" may have been a misnomer. Hitler and his mistress, Eva Braun, spent some time on a number of yachts on the Rhine, but very little time on any of them. He preferred his Alpine mountain retreat, Berchtesgaden. Disappointed with Germany's showing in the 1936 Berlin Olympics, Hitler ordered a series of racing vessels built. The *Ostwind* may have been one of them, but some marine historians believe the *Ostwind* started out as the *Grille* (German for "cricket") and was renamed when it was taken by the United States as a prize of war. The *Horst Wessel* was another of the wooden racing yachts Hitler had built. It was renamed *Eagle* and is now a training ship in the U.S. Coast Guard.

Heinrich Hoffman, Hitler's personal photographer, took photographs of Hitler and Eva Braun cruising the Rhine on board the *Grille/Ostwind*, but he knew the pictures were for the Fuhrer's personal album only and not for public consumption. Hitler did not wish to be seen swanning around on a luxury yacht, nor did he wish to be seen with Eva Braun.

Eva Braun had started out as Heinrich Hoffman's office assistant and became Hitler's mistress in 1932. He bought her a villa in Munich near his home and provided her with a chauffeured Mercedes. In 1936, she moved to Berchtesgaden and served as his chatelaine, out of sight of all but Hitler's intimates. The couple never appeared in public together and few Germans knew she existed. They were married in the Fuhrerbunker in 1945, a few hours before they committed suicide.

Hitler's favourite yacht was a steel-hulled tall ship owned by the Krupp munitions family. He used it for ceremonial occasions when presenting gallantry awards to German naval officers. Years later, the Krupp yacht turned up in St. Lucia re-named the *Yankee*.

West End resident, Don Miller, recalls taking a two-week "Barefoot Cruise" out of St. Lucia on the *Yankee* in the 1970s. "Barefoot cruises were intended for people who enjoyed sailing. I worked four hours on and eight off pulling ropes — putting sails up and taking them down. Our sleeping quarters were not luxurious; they were very basic, very Spartan. The food was exceptionally good. The captain was ex-British Navy. The majority of working passengers were couples. Our fares were on a par with or a little lower than conventional cruises."

With so many name changes to contend with, tracing Hitler's wooden windjammer racing yachts is like trying to nail jelly to a wall. None of the vessels turned up in searches of *Jane's Ships* or *Lloyd's Shipping Register*. To avoid paying port fees, some yachts mounted a gun on their fore deck to qualify as warships. *Jane's Fighting Ships* provides thumbnail information on these "armed yachts," but none of Hitler's tall ships are listed.

Bob Rodney worked as an office boy for J.A.D. McCurdy in aircraft supply and production during the war. When he took his holiday bus trip to New York, the Brooklyn navy yard was jammed with ships of all sizes and shapes — mothballed PT-Boats, landing craft, and gunboats. The *Queen Mary* rode at anchor. The *Grille* was dwarfed alongside her, and someone pointed out to Bob that it was Hitler's yacht.

He " had to photograph" the yacht. He was spotted by armed military police and chased away. Undeterred, he plotted a commando-type approach, over gangplanks and across the decks of acres of warships. The shore police gave chase again, but Bob managed a camera shot at a dead run.

Obviously, the U.S. Navy didn't want photos taken of "Hitler's yacht." Too many embarrassing questions might have been asked. General Dwight Eisenhower had appropriated the luxury yacht for his personal use and often entertained high-ranking military officers on Rhine cruises.

Marion Beasley has a photograph of her mother and aunt sailing on the Rhine "on Hitler's yacht." Her grandfather was the late Major General Robert John Fleming, Jr. who served as a colonel with the 1,140th Combat Engineer Group in Rhineland Province and the Ruhr Valley with the army of occupation.

"Hitler's yacht" was taken over by the U.S. Navy and then sold to a series of investors who hoped to turn it into a museum. The vessel ended up in storage for seven years at a Jacksonville, Florida, shipyard. When word got around it was "Hitler's yacht," vandals stripped her — including planking — for souvenirs. Others came to set the evil trophy of war on fire and destroy her. Pieces of the yacht's appointments, a mahogany art deco-style chair with original upholstery and a teakwood picture frame, turned up in a Virginia auction and were presented to Harrison Colket of the North American Smelting Co., Newark, Delaware. Mr. Colket took part in the salvage operation of the yacht just after the war ended.

J. J. Nelson, owner of the Florida shipyard, had to hire round the clock guards to ward off the thieving and the vengeful. The American Nazi Party tried to buy the tall ship and restore her, but Mr. Nelson decided it would be "more principled" to give her away to a Jewish group. Miami Commissioner Abe Resnick obtained permission from Dade County to scuttle the yacht 2.5 kilometres off shore. The derelict hull was transported from Jacksonville by a barge pulled by a tug captained by A. M. Daly, Jr.

Resnick was crammed, along with the 300 others, on the tiny *Florida Princess*. He was looking forward to wielding the sledgehammer that would free the wooden chocks and send "Hitler's yacht" to the bottom, 42 fathoms down. He was horrified when he saw Captain Daly swing the sledge and the hull went down at the wrong site — almost in the backyard of the famous Fontainebleau Hilton Hotel. Abe took the crossed signals in stride: "Hitler's soul is still somewhere there. I'm just kidding. It was truly an incredible, incredible historic event and suddenly ... BOOM! ... mistake," he added.

The miscue touched off a furious round of finger-pointing and name-calling. Abe Resnick blamed Captain Daly. The tugboat skipper blamed the master of the *Florida Princess,* Captain Chris Cadley. Abe Resnick said he would not pay to have the hull towed off the reef and sunk in deeper water. Nevertheless the Army Corps of Engineers gave the squabbling factions two weeks to get the job done or they would do it and bill Abe Resnick. He estimated the job would cost between $5,000 and $10,000. In the end, the Fontainebleau Hotel paid for the hull to be raised and resunk in deeper water. A hotel spokesman said: "the really sad thing was that in the two weeks the yacht was in shallow water divers defaced the wreck with anti-Semitic graffiti."

Chapter 11
Chevalier
Jerry Billing

T he Gospel of St. Matthew tells us that a prophet is not without honour, save in his own country. Jerry Billing is a minor god in Malta and Normandy and mainly unknown and ignored in Canada. He has probably seen more of life, death, and near-death than any other Canadian, yet, his 1995 nomination for the Order of Canada is buried somewhere in the Chancellery of Rideau Hall.

That same year, 1995, France knighted Jerry for his deeds in the air as a Spitfire fighter pilot over Normandy. The president of the Republic of France named him a *Chevalier dans l'Ordre National du Merite* (Knight of the Order of Merit) on the 50th anniversary of the end of World War II.

The Normandy town of Brehal awarded him their Medal

of Honour and made him an honorary citizen. The Island of Malta awarded him the Malta George Cross (commemorative 50th anniversary medal), and he was mentioned in dispatch. He wears four campaign stars — 1939–1945, Air Crew Europe, France and Germany, and Africa — and bars to two of them. Jerry flew more than 250 aerial combat sorties off Malta and over Normandy.

Billing was barely out of high school when he joined the RCAF in 1940. He had never been in the cockpit of an airplane. All that would soon change. The cocky kid from South Woodslee, Ontario, would soon be flying with George Beurling, "Hap" Kennedy, Stan Turner, Robert Hyndman, "Laddie" Lucas, and Johnny Johnson.

Malta was a key base in the Mediterranean: the Allies held it, Field Marshal Erwin Rommel wanted it, and German and Italian bombers and fighters pounded the island relentlessly on a daily basis. In fact, King George VI awarded the island of Malta a George Cross for its bravery in preventing the fortress from falling into enemy hands.

Life on Malta was a living hell for a fighter pilot. Fighter planes had to be flown in off aircraft carriers. The temperature was unbearable and rations were in short supply. Pilots suffered from "Malta Dog" (dysentery), and sand fleas made life miserable. Staple rations were a couple of slices of bread, hardtack biscuits, and gulls' eggs.

In 1943, Jerry destroyed a German Ju52 off the coast of Sicily, and much later another "probable" Ju52 kill was confirmed. He shot down a Ju88 over Normandy during the D-Day invasion.

"The Luftwaffe sent 13 Ju88 night fighters from the Bay of Biscay and we got them all but one. I closed in on one and while I was attacking, two crew members bailed out. I saw the Ju88 crash in the Orne River estuary." Some 35 years later, that Ju88 was found with the pilot still in it. Because of the place, time, two crew bailing out, and the French folk viewing the attack, the kill was confirmed. "Robert Hyndman of Old Chelsea, Quebec, was a Spitfire pilot himself in France and he painted an oil of my attack on the Ju88. It now hangs in the Bayeux Museum."

Museums in Malta and Bayeux display many pieces of Jerry's wartime memorabilia — his flight helmet, Mae West life jacket, tunic, boots, ribbons, and pieces of his Spitfires. There are even pieces of Jerry. When the two knees he banged up in his Normandy crash were replaced last year, he preserved pieces of bone in bottles of formaldehyde and sent them off to Bayeux Museum.

Jerry was shot down twice by enemy fighters over the Mediterranean and once by enemy flak over Normandy. He parachuted to the relative safety of a dinghy and was picked up by fast motor rescue launches. Floating under a parachute canopy or floating in a rubber raft were not always guarantees of safety. German and Italian fighters were known to machine gun pilots in the air or in their rafts.

Jerry's third crash landing was not as soft. His Spitfire

was travelling 258 kmph, when he executed a wheels-up landing. Cumberland doctor Hap Kennedy flew overheard in his Spit and gave Jerry landing tips and covering fire. Every Christmas since 1944, Hap has sent Jerry a card inscribed with his last radio transmission: "There's a good field off to your left wing. It looks long enough (to crash-land in)." A month later, Kennedy was shot down over Normandy, parachuted into occupied territory and, like Jerry, was befriended by a local farmer and the Marquis. He evaded capture for a month before linking up with U.S. forces.

Kennedy was awarded the Distinguished Flying Cross and bar. He destroyed 14 enemy aircraft and shared three other kills. His diary of a Spitfire fighter pilot, *Black Crosses Off My Wingtip*, is a classic chronicle of winged warfare. Hap was also overhead on one of the occasions Jerry had to bail out near Malta.

For a month, Jerry eluded German patrols that were searching for him. He hid in bulrushes and mud pools and ate grass and an occasional stolen cabbage. He brazenly walked past German sentries by playing a drooling village idiot. The Germans picked him up twice and twice he escaped from chicken coop jails. Once, he avoided capture by knifing a German soldier. Finally, he was befriended by an elderly farmer in Brehal, and the entire town of 2,500 sheltered him until he was liberated by U.S. troops weeks later. The underground provided false identity papers. Jerry was able to walk about and even drew rations from the Hun.

Very seldom did Jerry return to base with any unex-pended shells in his wing cannons. After one sortie, his "Erk" (rigger/technician) hopped on a wing and asked: "What'd you get, Jerry?"

"One church, one pill box, a train, a couple of Eyeties I know of and I hope that Jesus submarine blew up," he said. "Make it three Eyeties; I blew one off the sub."

The submarine attack happened just off Malta.

"I dove and at 300 feet I opened fire. His return fire was early and accurate. I could see tracer bullets coming at me. My bullets hit the sub's conning tire. I saw one sailor blown off the deck. I banked for another attack. I began firing 600 yards [549 m] out. I saw something explode within the con-ning tower. Climbing away, I looked back and saw the smok-ing craft. I headed for home because my fuel supply wasn't too good."

When Jerry talks of his daily dance with death, he becomes nostalgic. It was all over "just when I was getting the hang of it."

When the war ended, Jerry kept on flying. He taught fighter tactics on Sabre jets. He test-flew supersonic jets for two years in England, was a test pilot for DeHavilland in Europe on multi-engine aircraft, and he ferried planes to Vietnam. He has no idea how many hours he has logged in the air: "I've gone through four logbooks." He probably belongs in the Guinness Book of Records for his hours in the cockpit of a Spitfire. He flew a Spit for 52 years, 23 of them as movie actor Cliff Robertson's personal Spitfire pilot. Robertson bought a war surplus Spitfire for $60,000 and sold it to a Seattle aviation buff for $1.2 million U.S.

Robertson's plane — a Mark 1X Spitfire (serial number 923) — flew air cover with RAF 126 Squadron over Normandy on D-Day and shot down two ME109s. In 1961, it flew as an "extra" in the movie, *The Longest Day* while, on the ground, Robertson appeared in a starring role. Cliff Robertson has said that Jerry Billing was "a magnificent pilot, a brave and great patriot, a treasured friend, and one of the last true knights of battle." Jerry's romance with Spitfires ended in 1994 when he had two in-flight engine failures.

Jerry and his wife, Karen, and their two grandsons, Kyle and Mitchell, did a two-week tour of Normandy, courtesy of Michael Potter, with whom Jerry had worked in Ottawa. Once in France, Jerry and his family were guests of Brehal and the Bayeux Museum. There were no shortages of red carpets, complimentary hotel suites, limousines, and civic receptions. Normandy's "Canadian Knight" was home.

Jerry's wingmen back home in South Woodslee anxiously awaited his return. A gaggle of 30 to 40 Canada geese fly with him when he takes his 65 hp Aeronca up every day.

Chapter 12
Indiana Jones in the Royal Canadian Navy

is incredible real-life deeds make Indiana Jones look like Mary Poppins, yet few Canadians have ever heard of Commodore O.C.S. "Long Robbie" Robertson.

Owen Connor Struan "Robbie" Robertson was born in Victoria, British Columbia, on April 16, 1907. He wasn't called "Long Robbie" for nothing. He was six feet seven inches tall.

He first went to sea, "below decks," in 1924 as an ordinary seaman with the Canadian Government Merchant Marine. When World War II broke out, he was a lieutenant commander and captain of the HMCS *Fundy*. By 1943, he was commanding officer of the HMC Dockyard and king's harbour master in Halifax.

Indiana Jones in the Royal Canadian Navy

At 0720 hours on November 3, 1943, a U.S. freighter, SS *Volunteer*, was on fire in Halifax harbour. She was loaded with ammunition — 500 tons of light ammunition, 2,000 drums of highly combustible magnesium, 1,800 tons of heavy howitzer ammunition, depth charges, and cases of dynamite. Twenty-six years earlier the French munitions ship, *Mont Blanc*, blew up in Halifax harbour killing almost 2,000 people and wounding more than 4,000; 1,700 homes were destroyed and 12,000 were damaged. Few panes of glass remained in Halifax/Dartmouth. By way of comparison, the *Mont Blanc* was carrying 2,300 tons of picric acid, 200 tons of TNT, 10 tons of gun cotton, and 35 tons of benzol. The SS *Volunteer* had a potential for disaster equal to the original Halifax Explosion.

Long Robbie boarded the vessel and found most of the crew had abandoned ship and the officers were drunk. He donned an asbestos hood and oxygen mask and descended into the stokehold (compartment on a steamship housing boilers and furnaces) where the fire had started. Explosions began in number three hold.

Robertson asked the intoxicated ship's master for permission to flood number three hold and he refused. Long Robbie began rigging hose to flood the hold and called for the U.S. Naval Liaison Officer. Lieutenant Commander Stanley, U.S. Navy (USN), arrived, stripped the intoxicated captain of his command, took command himself, and turned it over to Robertson.

By this time, the fire had spread to number two hold. Robertson called for tugs and had the *Volunteer* towed to McNab Island, where he intended to open the sea cocks and scuttle the vessel off Mauger's Beach in a deep trough. But first, he had to deal with a build-up of cordite fumes that could blow any second. He ordered his firefighting party to stack bales of tobacco around the magnesium drums and cut holes in the main deck above the drums. Then, he fired a rifle at the magnesium drums and the resulting explosion snuffed out the fire. The holes he had ordered cut in the deck allowed flames and gases to escape. It was 1600 hours. A time bomb had been defused. For 8 hours and 40 minutes, Halifax had been on the brink of a second horrific disaster. Long Robbie Robertson was awarded the George Medal — one of seven (plus four bars) awarded to naval personnel in World War II.

Why only a George Medal? In 1866, a British Army private soldier, Timothy O'Hea, 20, extinguished a fire on a train travelling between Quebec and Montreal. A railway car carrying a ton of ammunition was uncoupled near Danville. Private O'Hea doused the fire with buckets of water. He was awarded a peacetime Victoria Cross. O'Hea saved a railway car, its cargo, and some nearby buildings. Long Robbie Robertson may have saved half of Halifax/Dartmouth.

His wartime heroism was not at an end by any means. Two years later, in July 1945, there was an explosion and fire in the Bedford magazines. The magazines were underground bunkers along the shoreline of Bedford Basin and extended for more than a half-kilometre. The concrete compartments held hundreds of thousands of tons of shells, torpedoes, ammunition, and TNT. Long Robbie was placed in command of the firefighting party that knocked the fire down. It took them four days. The Royal Canadian Navy credited him with averting "an unthinkable disaster."

On November 21, 1954, the HMCS *Labrador* entered Halifax harbour. The 6,500-ton modified wind class Arctic patrol vessel had just become the very first Canadian warship to circumnavigate North America and the first vessel to do it in a single voyage. The *Labrador* was the first warship to negotiate the Northwest Passage across the top of the world and return home by way of the Panama Canal. Her skipper was Captain O.C.S. Robertson.

The *Labrador* and the RCMP vessel *St. Roch* had a historic rendezvous off Point Atkinson. The *St. Roch* had navigated the Northwest Passage twice and, in 1950, circumnavigated North America. They sailed into Vancouver harbour together. The *St. Roch* went to a permanent home in a maritime museum. Robbie Robertson attended the vessel's transfer to Vancouver. Buglers from the *Labrador* gave her a final salute. She set course for the Panama Canal and home to Halifax.

Robbie had spent two years working and training with the U.S. Navy and Coast Guard before his voyage through the Northwest Passage. He had an excellent working relationship with the Americans. When he was attached to the U.S. Navy for polar operations, he was a crew member of the blimp *ZTG-2* during its voyage to Arctic ice island T-3 in 1958.

Then, he served as ice pilot aboard the U.S. submarine USS *Seadragon* during its underwater run of the Northwest Passage in 1960. He also served as ice pilot under the polar ice pack on board the U.S. submarine USS *Sargo*. One of his underwater voyages was to the North Pole in August/ September 1960. Thus, he became not only the very first naval officer to negotiate the Northwest Passage and circumnavigate North America — he also became the first person to sail through the Northwest Passage both on the surface and submerged.

I first saw this courtly and aloof officer in the wardroom, HMCS *Stadacona* officers' mess in Halifax in 1955. I was a second lieutenant in the Canadian Officers' Training Corps doing my third phase (summer) with Six Company Service Corps, Halifax.

"Stad" was the place to go on Friday evenings after 5 p.m. The mess offered "Penny Beer" — buy a draft for a dime and get a second one for a penny. You could buy a tray of drafts for 66 cents.

Lowly 90-day wonders (second lieutenants) didn't hobnob with captains and commodores with inches of gold braid on their sleeves. So, I didn't get to meet Long Robbie. But at six feet seven inches, he was hard to miss. Besides, navy wardrooms were reserved and stuffy ("pusser") officers' clubs

— totally opposite to the informal and sometimes rowdy army officers' mess, Royal Artillery Park, at the foot of the Halifax Citadel, where I lived.

Years later, we both worked at Expo '67, the 1967 Montreal World's Fair. I was a senior PR officer and Robbie was on loan as a scientific advisor. We chatted often and I had no idea I was in the presence of one of Canada's bravest heroes, because he never boasted, or even spoke of his achievements. He was named an Officer of the Order of Canada in June 1970. He passed away on November 22, 1994.

Fifty years ago, the *Labrador* slipped her moorings in Halifax and headed north. She carried an RCMP inspector, an RCMP constable and his family, 10 scientists, a ship's company of 225 officers and men, and a 17-member dog team.

After their conquest of the Northwest Passage, publicity shy Robbie Robertson and his crew were mobbed by press and public when they sailed into Esquimalt on September 27, 1954. They left there October 11, but before they sailed, under cover of darkness, they installed one of their 750-pound Arctic beacons on the reviewing officer's platform on the parade square. The next morning, the commodore had difficulty even finding enough footing to take the salute at ceremonial divisions.

Chapter 13
Polish Treasures in Wartime Canada

O n July 4, 1940, the MV *Batory*, the flagship of Poland's merchant fleet, upped anchor in the Clyde estuary. As the ship rounded Ailsa Craig ("Paddy's Milestone"), a 335-metre high volcanic hiccup halfway between Glasgow and Belfast, an escort of a Royal Navy battleship flanked by cruisers and destroyers joined her.

The *Batory* was carrying history's richest payload to Canada for wartime safekeeping. In her holds were a small fraction of Poland's state treasures and several hundred million dollars in precious metal — Bank of England gold bars destined for Bank of Canada vaults on Wellington Street. Britain did not want to chance the bullion falling into enemy hands if the island fell before an imminent German invasion.

When the convoy of one and her guardians sailed past head-lands or through "U-boat Alley," fighter planes, bombers, and flying boats flew protective air cover.

The cream of Poland's priceless heritage was packed in large custom-made trunks and long metal tubes. The value was beyond attaching monetary worth. The treasures includ-ed *Szczerbiec*, the jewelled coronation sword of Polish kings dating back to 1320, a two-volume Gutenberg Bible, 136 Flemish tapestries (some of which had been commissioned by a Polish king between 1549 and 1572), an aquamarine sceptre set in gold, the sword of the Order of the White Eagle and the chain of order last used at the coronation of King Stanislaus in 1764, prayer books and religious manuscripts from the 13th century, the oldest translation of psalms in the Polish language (a 14th century Florian psalter, the oldest pre-served Polish document), the 13th century Annals of the Holy Cross, 36 original Chopin compositions and 13 pieces of his correspondence, hundreds of pieces of gold and silver (cups, mugs, salvers, clocks, and suits of 17th century armour), and a 1608 chessboard that belonged to King Sigismund III.

Wawel Castle Museum staff knew a time would come for their national collection to go into hiding. Planning began when Hitler swallowed up Czechoslovakia. Six months later, on September 1, 1939, Heinkel planes dropped 48 tons of bombs on Cracow, the first bombs of World War II.

It was time.

The Polish army had to reconsider its pledge of transport. Bombing had interrupted rail transportation, and traffic on the Vistula River had been pre-empted by the military. The curators located a clapped-out 197-foot coal barge. They also found a wagon — but no horse — to take the cargo to the river just over two kilometres away.

Finally, they located a tractor. They worked all night and into the next day loading the treasures. Poling the barge down the Vistula by night, they ran without lights, hiding in the daytime by camouflaging their ungainly craft. The barge carried 82 passengers, museum staff, and their families. Embers fell on the deck as they floated under burning bridges. They drifted silently past German panzers growling on the riverbanks. When it became foolhardy to travel by water, the cargo was off-loaded onto a horse drawn wagon and taken to Lublin, 40 kilometres away. Luftwaffe fighters and dive-bombers strafed anything that moved at will. Running this gauntlet took more than two days.

The museum staff did not linger in Lublin. It had been bombed the previous evening. Fierce ground fighting raged to the north and west. The Polish army offered transport out. The convoy crossed the Dniesti River into neutral Rumania to Bucharest, where they found total confusion — a Tower of Babel passing for a Polish embassy. The curators were told there was no room at the inn — no storage space for the national treasures. The British embassy came to the rescue and offered a secure garage.

The Poles did not trust King Carol of Rumania, because

he was being pressured by Germany to impound the valu-
ables. They asked the apostolic delegate, the Papal Nuncio
in Bucharest, for sanctuary in Rome. The Vatican's answer
was a swift no. The items were judged to be secular without
sacred provenance.

The Polish government-in-exile in France ordered the
treasures brought there, so the cargo was transported by train
to Constanza on the Black Sea and loaded on the Rumanian
freighter *Ardeal*. The vessel passed through the Dardanelles
into the Aegean Sea, where it was stopped by a British
destroyer and escorted to a naval base at Malta.

The British suspected the ship was carrying barley
bound for Germany. But, Lady Luck finally intervened and
the *Ardeal* was permitted to continue. Poland's chief curator,
Dr. Stanislaw Swierz-Zaleski, was acquainted with Chevalier
Scicluna, director of archives for the Knights of Malta. The
chevalier was a friend of Malta's governor, General Bonham-
Carter, who used his rank to arrange for the ship's parole.

The *Ardeal* docked in Genoa on Christmas Day
1939. From there, the treasures travelled to Marseilles and
Aubusson, France. On May 19, 1940, the curators were
told France was no longer safe and to prepare to leave for
Bordeaux and England. The Polish coal ship, *Chorzow*, sailed
from Bordeaux on June 17 with 193 passengers, many of them
Polish fliers anxious to continue their fight against Germany
with the all-Polish fighter squadron at Northolt near London.
One of the ships alongside the *Chorzow* suffered a direct

hit from a German bomb, and the *Chorzow's* captain broke away from the flotilla, making it safely to Falmouth, England — alone and unescorted.

The journey of the treasures was far from over. From Falmouth they were sent by rail to London and stored in the Polish embassy at 47 Portland Place. Their stay there was short, because London was under siege; the Battle of Britain had begun, and Britain was preparing for an invasion. With the approval of Ottawa, the Canadian High Commission told the curators the collection was being offered sanctuary in Canada, with one condition: once in Canada, the artifacts and tapestries would be the responsibility of their Polish minders.

The treasures travelled by rail to the Clyde port of Greenock and were placed in the hold of the *Batory*. The *Batory* docked at Pier 20 in Halifax on July 13, 1940. Along with the artifacts and gold bullion, she was carrying a manifest even more precious — hundreds of Jewish children who were being billeted by Canadian Jewish families. The Royal Canadian Mounted Police and Halifax dockyard police threw a tight security screen around the freight shed on Pier 20. The trunks, crates, and tubes were placed in sealed rail cars. Two days later, they arrived in Ottawa and were taken immediately to the Polish Consulate General on Stewart Street.

The director of the national archives, Dr. Gustave Lanctot, offered free secure storage space in the archives records storage building at the Experimental Farm. The treasures were moved in. Tapestries were unfurled and hung from overhead rods. Two skilled Polish-Canadian weavers from Ottawa, Mrs. Martha Kozlowska and Mrs. Franciszka, were commissioned to repair and restore them over the next nine months. By this time, Poland had ceased to be a nation. The country was under German occupation, and the Polish government was in exile in London. In their wildest dreams, no one thought that more than 20 years would pass before the art treasures would be returned to Wawel Castle.

The forced march through Europe was a minor skirmish compared to the vicious infighting that was ahead. Duplicity and intrigue were matches for any Graham Greene novel plot. The skirmishes blackened Canada's name at the United Nations, at UNESCO, on the floor of the House of Commons, at Canadian Polish Congress councils, and in the Polish press. There were threats of an action in the International Court of Justice in The Hague. Throughout it all, Canada was an innocent player, but kept getting hit by ricochets from rounds fired by the communist government in Warsaw, the Polish government-in-exile in London, and Polish émigrés in Canada and the United States.

The squabble over who held legal title to the treasures plagued four Canadian prime ministers, four Quebec premiers, four cardinal princes of the Catholic church, a secretary general of the United Nations, and senior Canadian mandarins such as Charles Ritchie, A.D.P. Heeney, Escott Reid, Jules Leger, H. L. Keenlyside, Henry Davis, Pierre Dupuy, Laval Fortier, Peter Dobell, R.A.D. Ford, and Jack Pickersgill, then a back room operative in Prime Minister Mackenzie King's office.

Four secretaries of state for external affairs — Louis St. Laurent, Lester B. Pearson, Sidney Smith, and Howard Green — were dragged into what was a dispute between warring Poles over ownership. Three other cabinet ministers — J. L. Ilsley, Donald M. Fleming, and Davie Fulton — also became reluctant pawns in the 20-year tug of war.

Poland's ambassador, Eugeniusz Milnikiel, referred to as "Minister of the Polish Republic" by the Communist regime in Warsaw, asked his government to recall him. After two years, he said he was "tired of the uselessness of his efforts and unchanging attitude of the Canadian government."

Despite the fact that Poland's national treasures had a fixed address at the Experimental Farm, some of them soon went absent without leave. Two locked and sealed trunks containing the Gutenberg Bible, the priceless coronation sword, and the Chopin manuscripts and correspondence were spirited away from the Farm and lodged with the Bank of Montreal on Sparks Street by custodians Dr. Swierz-Zaleski and Jospeh Polkowski. Nineteen years later the one surviving trustee agreed to release the trunks and "save harmless" the Bank of Montreal and the Canadian government. But it was only through intervention by Witold Malcuznyski, a leading Polish pianist and exponent of Chopin's music, that the trunks were returned to Poland in 1959 for the 150th anniversary of the composer's birth.

When the trunks left the bank on January 18, 1959, the RCMP and four Polish diplomatic couriers escorted the security van to Union Station. They were placed in a special railway car, which took them to New York to join the Swedish ship *Stockholm*. The two trunks were insured for $100 million, but the contents were priceless. They arrived in Warsaw in a sealed railway car on February 3. The Chopin items were placed on display before being returned to Wawel Castle, where 82,500 people viewed them over five days.

Meanwhile, back in Ottawa, more relics vanished. Eight trunks were hidden in the convent of the Sisters of the Precious Blood at 774 Echo Drive. The monastery, built in 1917, is a major architectural landmark across the Rideau Canal from Lansdowne Park. It was occupied by a community of nuns from 1917 to 1991, when it was sold to the Royal College of Physicians and Surgeons of Canada. The nuns insisted on security precautions — a receipt and the password, "The Holy Virgin of Czstochova." The clandestine move came at or about the time Canada was poised to recognize the new communist government in Warsaw. Despite the nuns' attempt at security, when Dr. Swierz-Zaleski came calling, the two trunks were missing. They had been removed two or three days earlier by "persons who knew the password."

The parish priest of the Polish community of Wilno and his custodian, E. Kozar, came under suspicion. Four cases weighing 481 kilograms were delivered to St. Mary's Church. The priest and custodian claimed the boxes contained "stucco composition." The federal government considered a search warrant and the Department of External Affairs asked Justice Minister J. L. Ilsley to "instruct the RCMP Commissioner to conduct an investigation to locate missing treasures."

The search warrant against Father E. Wilowski and his custodian (variously described in External Affairs memos as a "displaced person" or as a "DP") was never executed, since to pursue it would have strengthened the Polish claim that Canada was responsible for care and control. External Affairs files, three feet of onion skins and yellowing clippings stamped SECRET, were declassified a half-century later when I applied for access. The files reveal that the RCMP questioned personnel at the Toronto Art Gallery, Capital Storage Company of Ottawa, the Bank of Montreal, a Redemptorist Monastery in Ste-Anne-de-Beaupre, Hotel Dieu Convent in Quebec City, and the Convent of the Precious Blood on Echo Drive.

Quebec's premier, Maurice LeNoblet Duplessis, reacted with fury. He issued a press release condemning the RCMP who "without search warrants and in an illegal manner forced their way not only into the convent of the Sisters of Hotel Dieu but also into their cloister." The truth was that the Mounties did present themselves at Hotel Dieu without warrants, but the nuns volunteered to show them around.

Duplessis' press release was enough to bring the Conservative opposition member of Parliament for Lake Centre, John Diefenbaker, to his feet during Question Period.

He demanded that the minister of justice table the RCMP reports. The minister refused. Quebec's Cardinal Villeneuve entered the fray and ordered the sister superior at Ste-Anne-de-Beaupre to surrender the 23 trunks deposited there. Duplessis had the trunks impounded and placed behind locked doors in the Provincial Museum. Armed guards were stationed outside. Frosty relations between Ottawa and Quebec became frostier. Duplessis told Canada's Consul in Boston, Paul Beaulieu, he did not recognize the post-war Polish government.

The Polish embassy sent External Affairs a strongly worded diplomatic note charging Canada had lost control of the collection and was unaware of its whereabouts. A later, equally strong note held Canada responsible for the collection's deteriorating condition.

Duplessis' paper war was far from over. He issued another press release vowing, "No deal, agreement or compromise will ever be made with the contemptible Communist Government of Poland for their return." Duplessis said he would not surrender the treasures until "a competent court" established ownership.

The fire fight was not confined to government against government. The Catholic church and some private individuals came forward claiming ownership. Countess Tarnowska claimed a golden goblet. A Belgian citizen claimed the coronation sword. The sword was once booty captured by Russia in 1795. It surfaced again in Paris in 1864 in the possession of a private collector and was purchased by Russian principals and donated to the Hermitage Museum in St. Petersburg. The 1921 Treaty of Riga repatriated it to the Polish State. The Vatican's Papal Nuncio in Ottawa, Most Reverend Ildebrando Antonuitti, claimed a valuable Burgundy Arras tapestry (the Lohengrin Legend), the Gutenberg Bible, and several lesser items for the Catholic church in Poland.

Lester Pearson wrote in a memo to Prime Minister Louis St. Laurent: Canada "has no obligation to return to the Polish State the part of the collection [that has] not been impounded by Duplessis." Maurice Duplessis died suddenly on a visit to Schefferville. His successor, Paul Sauve, was more flexible and worked towards repatriating the collection. He died after a short time in office, as did his successor, Antonio Barrette. It was left to Liberal Premier Jean Lesage to square the circle.

On January 21, 1961, the last of the treasures left Ottawa in two heavily guarded security vans. The RCMP rode shotgun. At Rock Island, Vermont, state troopers took over and escorted the trucks through Vermont, New Hampshire, and Massachusetts to the port of Boston. The value placed on the artifacts was so huge that 28 insurance companies from France, England, Sweden, Japan, Mexico, Egypt, Russia, and the United States formed a consortium to amortize the risk of losses or damage during the ocean crossing.

The Polish art treasures were finally going home. But, did they all make the boat ride? Canada was never provided with an inventory. When the trunks in the Bank of Montreal were opened, the original seals had been tampered with. The inventory that was supposed to be inside was missing. Four rugs ended up in the Ottawa home of a senior member of the Polish legation. Who removed eight trunks from the Convent of the Sisters of the Precious Blood on Echo Drive and where were they taken when they "ostensibly disappeared?"

Fifty-year-old files reveal that 33 trunks were landed in Canada. The two trunks in the Bank of Montreal were returned to Poland in 1959. When the *Krynica* sailed from Boston to Poland in 1961 there were only 24 trunks on her manifest.

Are some Polish art treasures still in Canada?

Chapter 14
He Missed the Boat

The first published casualty reports of a 1942 torpedoing in the Gulf of St. Lawrence off Gaspe indicated that V-33301, Rating Philip Francis Brady, age 34, from Montreal, a member of the Royal Canadian Navy Volunteer Reserve, was missing in action and presumed lost at sea.

Reports of Brady's death were greatly exaggerated. He was not on board the armed yacht HMCS *Raccoon*, when a single torpedo from U-165 killed the entire crew of 37 and reduced the converted luxury boat to scrap.

Philip Francis Brady had missed the boat.

In the early morning of September 5, 1942, about 1 a.m., Brady was walking along the road when he was hit from behind by a car. The Fort Ramsay medical officer's report reads: "He had not been drinking and was returning to his ship ... He lost consciousness coming to the hospital." He suffered "abrasions about his face, considerable swelling at the bridge of his nose ... left little finger and left hand showed bruises ... no apparent fractures ... bruising on his left foot." X-rays confirmed there were no fractures. Brady would remain a patient in the hospital in Gaspe for nine days.

His ship, however, sailed the next day, September 6. The HMCS *Raccoon* was part of an escort for convoy QS 33 (Quebec to Sydney). A few days earlier, lookouts had seen the unmistakable white furrows of two torpedoes under the *Raccoon*'s bow. The U-boat commander failed to account for the *Raccoon*'s shallow draft, and his torpedo settings were too deep.

The *Raccoon*, the corvette HMCS *Arrowhead*, the minesweeper HMCS *Truro*, and Fairmile motor launches Q065 and Q083 were riding shotgun on eight merchant ships en route to Sydney. The Greek freighter *Aeas* was hit by a single torpedo from U-165 and sank immediately. As the convoy rounded Riviere-la-Madeleine, an explosion rocked the night at 1 a.m. on September 7. The other escort ships presumed it was from a depth charge dropped by the *Raccoon*. Much later, they learned the explosion was from a torpedo that blew the *Raccoon* to smithereens. That same day U-517 sent three more merchant ships to the bottom.

From that point on, Quebec-Sydney convoys were halted and war matériel bound for eastern Canadian ports and from there to Europe was moved by rail through Maine, New Brunswick, and Nova Scotia.

The Battle of the St. Lawrence wasn't a level playing field. The Canadian navy was unprepared to deal with a superior force of German submarines. Two U-boats sank 22 ships in the Gulf and not a single U-boat was lost. In June 1942, one U-boat sank four ships in broad daylight between Matane and Saint-Anne-des-Monts. Early in the war, Canada had one minesweeper and two Fairmiles responsible for patrolling the entire Gulf and St. Lawrence River. Fairmiles had little more than a three-foot draft and bobbed like corks.

Canadian warships had primitive sound detectors, puny deck guns, almost non-existent communications systems, and roll-off depth charges. Sub-chasers dropping depth charges had to pass directly over a submerged U-boat and had a six-percent success rate. A year later, some ships were equipped with British Hedgehogs, a 34-kilogram mortar bomb filled with 14 kilograms of TNT. Twenty-four Hedgehogs could be launched about 183 metres in an oval pattern. Hedgehogs exploded on contact. Even so, the Hedgehog's success rate was only 14 percent.

Depth charges were both a blessing and a curse. When the corvette *Charlottetown* was torpedoed, depth charges rolled off her stern and exploded among Canadian survivors struggling in the water. The blast concussion broke blood vessels, and sailors died a slow and painful death.

German propagandists scoffed that "nine-tenths [of

the Canadian navy] was composed of requisitioned fishing boats, coastal ships, and luxury yachts." The Canadian navy establishment was, indeed, merely token. Most members of the Royal Canadian Naval Reserve (RCNR) and the Royal Canadian Naval Volunteer Reserve (RCNVR) had only dry-land training in inner towns and cities and on the Prairies. Regular navy officers wore straight gold rank stripes. RCNVR officers wore zigzag braid and earned themselves the nickname of "wavy navy." Some anonymous wit once said the RCNVR were gentlemen trying to be sailors; the RCNR were sailors trying to be gentlemen and the RCN were neither, trying to be both.

Philip Francis Brady enlisted in the RCNVR in September 1941. His trade as an electrician probably landed him on the *Raccoon* to bring her electrical system up to standards. Brady served on board the HMCS *Montreal* and at Stadacona and Cornwallis before being posted to Fort Ramsay and the *Raccoon* on August 4, 1942.

Canada had one radar station located at Herring Cove near Halifax. A second primitive installation was built on the Gaspe coast — Fort Ramsay. A young signals officer stationed there was Sub-Lieutenant Murray Westgate who later became "your friendly Esso dealer" on Hockey Night in Canada.

The *Raccoon* had been built by a shipyard in Bath, Maine, in 1931 for wealthy U.S. businessman, Charles A. Thorne. In June 1931, she was christened *Halonia*. Thorne sold the steel-hulled schooner to the VanCleef family (of

VanCleef and Arpel jewellers) and, when war broke out and the United States was neutral, the VanCleefs sailed the *Halonia* from Cape Cod to Lake Ontario and donated the pleasure craft to the Canadian navy.

The *Halonia* was a twin-master schooner roughly the same size as the *Bluenose*. Dockyards in Saint John and Halifax were swamped with work so the *Halonia* sailed to Pictou, Nova Scotia, where the masts were removed. From there she went to the International Paper Company in Dalhousie, New Brunswick, where she was fitted with twin diesel engines and prepared for war. She was commissioned *Raccoon* and joined a dozen or so sister armed yachts for coastal patrol — the *Grizzly*, the *Beaver*, the *Caribou*, the *Cougar*, the *Elk*, the *Reindeer*, the *Musky*, and the *Wolf*. Some of the armed yachts were only 23 feet long.

The Canadian navy was ill prepared for combat. The first two of 14 corvettes had no guns in their turrets, so wooden posts were stuck in to present a silhouette that might scare off the German wolf pack. Canada also had 20 Fairmiles, 112-foot-long PT type boats — wooden sub chasers. A Fairmile carried a three-pounder gun on deck, depth charges, and Hedgehogs. They were powered by 1200 hp gasoline engines, which made them unsafe. A spark could ignite high-octane fumes, as happened once when a ship's cook lit a galley stove. The Fairmile blew up, killing two crew members. At its peak, Germany was building one U-boat every day.

In September 1942, a U-boat fired a fish at the freighter

Meadcliffe Hall and missed. The torpedo kept on going until it hit the beach where it exploded, breaking and rattling windows in the Quebec village of St. Yvon over one kilometre away. Sending the flimsy craft out to protect convoys and hunt down U-boats was akin to sending a boy on a man's errand.

After the torpedo struck the *Raccoon*, an RCAF spotter plane sighted a life preserver with "Halonia" stencilled on it and two Carley floats — all of the *Raccoon* that was ever recovered. The only body recovered was found washed ashore on Anticosti Island a month later. It was Russ McConnell, a Royal Roads graduate and a promising pro prospect in the Montreal Royals/Canadiens system. Russ McConnell was wrapped in a weighted shroud and buried at sea five kilometres off Gaspe.

The night the *Raccoon* went down, Mike Sheflin, retired Ottawa-Carleton transportation commissioner, was three years old. His father, John Edward "Jack" Sheflin, was a supply assistant on the *Raccoon*. Mike, his mother and five-year-old brother, Jim, were on board CN's Ocean Limited, rolling along the St. Lawrence. They were going home to Eureka in Pictou County so that Peggy and the boys would be closer to Halifax when the *Raccoon* docked. The Sheflins could not even see the St. Lawrence, because train conductors had orders to ensure all blinds were pulled down when lights were on so as not to present a target for U-boat deck guns.

Mike Sheflin says he believes that if he had looked out the train window the night of September 7 as the train rolled past Mont-Joli, he might have caught a glimpse of the *Raccoon* on the way to her rendezvous with death. A week after the *Raccoon* was torpedoed, the Sheflins received a telegram stating John Edward Sheflin was "missing and believed lost at sea." Peggy received an insensitive form letter addressed "To the Next of Kin of" that was machine signed by Angus L. Macdonald, Minister of National Defence for Naval Affairs. A month later on October 17, another letter arrived informing her she had been awarded a monthly pension of $87 for herself and her two children. Newspaper coverage was heavily censored. A press release simply stated: the *Raccoon* was "torpedoed in northern waters where enemy subs have been active."

U-165 met her end three weeks after sinking the *Raccoon*. She was sunk in the Bay of Biscay with all (51) hands lost. Philip Francis Brady's next postings were to Stadacona and Shelburne, Nova Scotia. He was demobilized July 13, 1945, and given a rehabilitation grant and a $100 "Plain Clothes Gratuity." He died April 18, 1961, at the age of 53. Peggy Sheflin passed away September 7, 1988, 46 years to the day her husband's life was snatched from her.

Chapter 15
Military Secrets

S ecrets have a way of justifying themselves beyond the point of necessity. Sometimes, especially in wartime, the military's need for or obsession with secrecy is understandable. Other times, it is downright ludicrous. Still, on other occasions, a mission has been kept secret for so long it becomes firmly wedged between the dusty cracks of history and the forgotten. The Official Secrets Act became a handy catchall, but a much abused legal instrument.

In May 1943, Guy Gibson's RAF Dambuster squadron flattened hydroelectric dams in Germany's Ruhr Valley. The daring nighttime raid was largely a military success and a tremendous morale booster for the Allied war effort. But it was not without great sacrifice. Nine of 19 raiders, each with a seven-man crew, were lost. The very next day, the RAF sent up a specially equipped photo reconnaissance Spitfire to film the damage. The plane carried no armament and flew above 30,000 feet. The name of the RAF pilot who flew the Spitfire was kept secret.

Peter Elliott, Senior Keeper of the Royal Air Force Museum in Hendon, England, e-mailed me to suggest "the identity of the pilot would not have been revealed during the war for security reasons and to protect him if he were subsequently taken prisoner." However, Peter Elliott went on to say, "I think it is highly unlikely that the RAF would deliberately suppress his name after the war — his flight should be recorded in his unit's operations record book, which will have been open for inspection in the National Archives since the mid-1970s."

Sounds reasonable. However, the RAF kept this pilot's name secret for 60 years. He is in his early 80s and alive and well in Oxfordshire. Several months ago he was interviewed by a *Daily Telegraph* writer and recalled his flight over the dams.

A Canadian Mosquito pilot, the late William John "Bill" O'Connell, Ottawa, fell afoul of military secrecy in November 1943. He was flying a Mark VI Mosquito with 21 Squadron, RAF, and was nearing the end of his second tour of operations. He was leading a two-plane, low-level attack against a power station at Cleve, a small city in northwest Germany a few kilometres beyond the Dutch border. They planned to cross the Dutch coast at 12:05 noon, in a sector they had flown over the previous day. Then, there "wasn't a sign of a German gun anywhere." When they were still 6.4 kilometres out at sea, German ack-ack guns began firing at them at a fairly long range. The fire originated from an arc between their 10 o'clock position and their 2 o'clock.

Bill O'Connell began eyeballing the ground at 12 o'clock for an explanation for the firepower. Was the German ground battery protecting something new? O'Connell saw a low building that was a recent addition to the coast.

"Had the Germans not drawn our attention to the site with the gun-fire, there was a pretty good chance that we would have missed it." He opened fire 1,829 metres away and poured 20 mm cannon bursts at the structure and machine gun fire as his range closed. When he had exhausted his ammunition he flew directly over the building and noted a vast amount of grey smoke and tangled antennae wires. Returning to base in Hunsden, Hertfordshire, he found himself in very deep doo-doo because he had abandoned the attack on his primary target. His Mosquito had suffered only one hit; a solid-ball 20 mm cannon shell had penetrated his starboard engine nacelle and punctured a tire on the right wheel. The undercarriage was intact and he managed to safely land the crippled plane, still carrying four 227-kilogram bombs. His senior officer raked him over the coals: "Why didn't you go to Cleve as you had been briefed?" He dismissed the attack as "humph, a fish hut or something! You should know that there are no German radar stations in Holland."

A few days later, while debriefing O'Connell, a junior operations officer told him he had tried to pursue the attack for intelligence reasons, but had been ordered to "forget it."

"A day or two later, that same junior officer sought me out in the officers' mess and said they had received a message from the Dutch resistance about your operation. Group headquarters asked if we had any aircraft from 140 Wing on operations on November 30. Group was told 'no, we had no aircraft on operations on that date.' I should point out that two totally fictitious and consecutive entries appear in 21 Squadron Operations Record Book. Arthur [his navigator] and I are on record as the crew that failed to make an accurate landfall ... at the Dutch coast. The fact is we were dead on track. We never missed a landfall. Someone seemed to be trying to represent to history that Arthur and I were an incompetent crew.

"No one at group headquarters would ever know that an aircraft of 21 Squadron got a tire shot out while it was not officially on operations."

Years later, Bill O'Connell learned that the low building he destroyed was a key German Over-the-Horizon (O-T-H) radar installation. Single-handedly, he may have been responsible for crippling German plans to strengthen fortress Europe. Over-the-Horizon radar was a key element in their grand design. Bill O'Connell's "target of opportunity" attack destroyed an experimental station and killed 16 technicians and soldiers.

"Did we change history that day? By reducing the German O-T-H radar to rubble, had we, in fact, also ensured the success of the Allied landings in Normandy on D-Day? It could well have been. With O-T-H radar near Calais, the Germans could have negated the sham force at Dover and they would have been able, perhaps, to pick up the true invasion force on the south coast of England."

Bill O'Connell has "exchanged correspondence with Dr. Theo Boiten, a young Dutch historian who was writing a book entitled, *Blenheim Strike.*" Dr. Boiten unearthed oral confirmation from resistance members that a radar station had been destroyed in an attack on November 30, 1943. A Dutch lady who had dated a young German anti-Nazi naval officer when she was a girl, volunteered that the officer told her a major device for detecting aircraft had been destroyed and "created a great deal of concern among the German officers." Another Dutch citizen who had been pressed into service as a German messenger was 91 metres from the building and saw two German soldiers get blown away. But he didn't know what was in the building. So, there is no official or unofficial corroboration that the building was a radar base. There are no ULTRA code breakers' reports in British defence department archives. Dr. Boiten's contacts could not find copies of any resistance messages in the Dutch National Archives in Amsterdam.

Bill O'Connell wrote to German War Archives in Berlin and was told there was no record of a Mosquito attack on

November 30, 1943. RAF records for station Sculthorpe in British archives are incomplete. Bill O'Connell maintains the names of two out of four operations room staff officers are missing. One name missing is that of the senior operations officer (OPSO).

"If he is still alive, maybe he could throw some light on these questions if he chose to do so. Or it may well be that the name of the other officer missing from the staff at Sculthorpe was the junior officer who approached me twice asking my permission to pursue a conclusion to our attack on a German radar unit. He's the one who was told to 'forget it.'

"Over the years, I have become more and more convinced that our target on November 30, 1943, had indeed been the world's first O-T-H radar and the very first target that showed on their screens was ironically the last." Bill O'Connell may never know if his strike shortened the war and guaranteed the success of the D-Day landings.

Official secrets, you know!

Chapter 16
Smokey and Me

Ernest "Smokey" Smith was the last living Canadian to wear the Victoria Cross (VC). Sixteen Canadians won a VC during World War II. Smokey was the only private soldier. He went through war and life "raising hell." Smokey did for good order and discipline what Don Cherry does for grammar and diction. He was promoted to corporal nine times and "busted" back to private nine times. It was fortuitous that he was awarded the Victoria Cross. He couldn't win a good conduct medal if he lived to be 150.

Smokey was built like a fire-plug: short, stocky, barrel-chested, muscular, and powerful. He didn't go looking for fights, but he never backed away from one. He didn't look for trouble. Trouble looked for him. He was like Joe Bfstplk in the

L'il Abner comic strip. Joe Bfstplk walked about with his own personal black rain cloud over his head.

Smokey got to Europe the hard way, as a Seaforth Highlander hitting a beach in Sicily. He was seriously wounded and not expected to live when fragments from a rifle grenade hit him. He recovered, fought his way up the boot of Italy, and survived Ortona and the Hitler Line battles. The night of October 21/22, 1944, he won his VC "raising hell" against a German mechanized unit.

Smokey and two Highlanders had been sent ahead across the Savio River to establish a beachhead. During a torrential rainstorm, the river level rose 1.8 metres in a few hours. They were cut off. They found themselves facing three Mk V Panther tanks, two self-propelled guns, and 30 German infantry soldiers. At point-blank range, 9 metres from his target, Smokey fired a PIAT (Projector, Infantry, Anti-Tank) rocket and took out a tank. He mowed down advancing German soldiers with a Tommy gun and then destroyed a second tank and both self-propelled guns, all the while shielding a badly wounded comrade. He fired every weapon he could lay his hands on. "I was firing PIATs from the hip," he later recounted. Smokey told me the Germans thought they were up against at least a platoon. The surviving Germans retreated.

In December 1944, Smokey was told to pack his kit. He was going to Naples. Upon arriving in Naples he was locked in the guardhouse. He would not be allowed on the loose to sample the juices of local vineyards. He was also told he was going to receive the Victoria Cross from King George VI at Buckingham Palace. When he arrived in London, however, he was locked up again until shortly before the ceremony. There would be no English pub crawl.

After the war, the City of New Westminster established an annuity for him and he started up a travel agency. Retired Ottawa travel agent, Ray Sally, met Smokey in the 1960s. They were on a British Airways (BA), all expenses paid, 30-day familiarization junket to Fiji, New Zealand, and Australia. Ray recalls that, before departure, BA hosted a farewell cocktail party in a Los Angeles hotel suite.

"I overheard one lady say to another: 'I'm really looking forward to this trip now that that horrible Mr. Smith won't be with us.' I was curious, so I asked who Mr. Smith was and where he was. She told me he was passed out in one of the bedrooms of the suite. So, I woke him up, got him on the plane and we've been fast friends ever since." The pair cut a wide swath on the "fam junket."

"One night," Sally further recalled, "BA hosted a dinner/dance and after dinner, the band struck up a conga tune. We all got out on the floor, and the next thing I heard was a lady saying to her husband 'do you know what that horrible man just did?' Smokey was in the conga line and maybe his hands slipped down a little from the lady's waist. The next thing we knew we were on our asses outside. When the German manager of a night club attempted to curb his boisterous conduct,

Smokey told him what he had done to 30 Germans in World War II: 'You'd take me all of 10 seconds,' he boasted."

Smokey took delight in wearing the maroon VC ribbon. All ranks, from field marshal down, are required to salute the medal. If Smokey saw a pair of red collar tabs across a parade square, he'd walk hundreds of metres out of his way to intercept the officer. If the officer didn't salute, Smokey would tap the ribbon with his finger until the officer got the message.

He brought a firestorm down on his head during a royal visit. Queen Elizabeth noticed his miniature VC and paused to speak. Afterwards, he was scrummed by media and asked if he was nervous when the Queen spoke to him.

"Naw," Smokey replied. "When you've met one you've met them all." It became the banner headline in the next day's newspapers. West Coast monarchists went ape. Broadcaster Jack Webster pulled Smokey's chestnuts out of the fire on his radio show: "You didn't say that, did you, Smokey? You must have been misquoted." Smokey agreed.

He was invited to attend a mess dinner and to sit at a head table with Lieutenant Colonel Cecil Merritt, another VC recipient. Smokey said, "You have a portrait of Cece Merritt hanging over your bar. Put my picture up alongside his and I'll come."

"But, Smith, you're only a private. This is an officers' mess."

"Makes no difference. If you don't put my picture up I'm not coming."

Smokey and Me

The picture went up.

In the early 1970s, Smokey and I linked up for three days in London where he was attending a VC reunion. I had met him through Ray Sally in Ottawa a week earlier when the three of us put a fair dent in a keg of cold draft at Sammy Koffman's Belle Claire Hotel one Saturday afternoon. I was just off the plane from Canada and checking in at the Kingsley Hotel in Bloomsbury Way when the desk clerk said there was a call for me. It was Smokey. He was on his way over. For the next three days, we terrorized High Holborn, Piccadilly, and Mayfair. The man had the constitution of a canal horse and refused to accept there was such a medical condition as a hangover.

We came back to the Kingsley from a ceremony at St. Martin-in-the-fields Church one noon and repaired to the saloon bar. Smokey was wearing his miniatures. A well dressed Brit approached, excused himself for interrupting, and asked: "Is that the 'effing' Victoria Cross?" Smokey allowed that it "effing" well was and, from that moment on, we couldn't buy another drink. The Dom Perignon flowed until closing time. I have no recollection of being put to bed. The next morning my stomach was returning drop kicks to my head and there was Smokey — tucking into a full-cooked English breakfast.

That evening I went to the Cafe Royale on Piccadilly to help Smokey make an early getaway from a stuffy dinner. Princess Anne was at the head table and Smokey was sitting next to her. Before I could tell him I had a (phony) "urgent message" for him, he turned to the Princess Royal and asked: "Your Highness, have you met Pat MacAdam from Glace Bay?" The Princess looked as if she had been struck between the eyes with an axe handle. She hadn't the foggiest idea who I was and I am sure she didn't know what a Glace Bay was.

Smokey left with me and off we went into the night looking for new territories to conquer. Somewhere along the route we linked up with an off duty bobby, a Soho publican, and a retired British Army major whose service in India was guarding a maharajah's tigers. I was awakened next morning by pounding. I hoped it wasn't my head. It was my hotel room door. There, booted and spurred in full uniform, was our bobby friend. He was carrying a couple of cold cans of best bitter. There is a Santa Claus.

Smokey never entered a bar; he stormed it. But he was a warm human being, always entertaining and always fun to be with. There was never a dull moment travelling with Smokey Smith.

Chapter 17
Canada's Most Decorated Hero of WWII

Canada's most decorated World War II hero, Johnnie Fauquier, was buried in Ottawa's Beechwood Cemetery with full military honours more than a quarter century ago, and then forgotten. Only family members and a few fellow wartime bomber crews remember him.

Had Johnnie Fauquier been an American, Hollywood might have passed over Audie Murphy, Congressional Medal of Honor winner and the United States' most decorated soldier, for star treatment. The movie *To Hell and Back*, which starred Audie Murphy himself, told the story of his heroism.

Johnnie Fauquier went to hell and back almost 100 times on bombing raids over Berlin, other key German targets, and the Peenamunde V2 rocket bases on the Baltic Sea. The normal tour for a bomber pilot was 30 raids. He did three tours and then some. He was the first Canadian to command a bomber squadron in battle, commanding both the crack RCAF 405 Pathfinder Squadron and later the RAF's legendary Dambusters. Johnnie Fauquier was awarded the Distinguished Service Order Medal (second only to the Victoria Cross) three times — more than any other Canadian warrior. He also wore the distinctive ribbon of the Distinguished Flying Cross on his tunic.

It is unlikely that Audie Murphy would have even been considered for the role of Johnnie Fauquier in a movie. Errol Flynn, Clark Gable, Douglas Fairbanks, or Jimmy Cagney would have been elbowing one another aside to play him in a film, such were his exploits as "King of the Pathfinders" and totally fearless bomber pilot.

The Fauquiers were French Huguenots who probably came to North America to fight with Lafayette against the British at the Battle of New Orleans. There is also an old established Fauquier County in the Commonwealth of Virginia.

John Emilius Fauquier was born in Ottawa in 1909 with a silver spoon in his mouth. His father, Gilbert Emilius, was a wealthy construction tycoon who built the Ontario leg of the first trans-continental railway. The Fauquier family home in Rockcliffe on Manor Road is now the residence of the Swedish ambassador.

Johnnie attended Ashbury College and became head prefect. He was a top student and, in athletics, he won more than 40 soccer, rugby, and cricket trophies. He moved to Montreal and became a successful but reluctant St. James' Street stockbroker. His family's standing in Ottawa social circles helped him move freely among Montreal's finest. To blunt the tedium of his day job, he raced fast cars and motorcycles. Then, he took flying lessons at the Montreal Light Aeroplane Club. The die was cast. He was a natural pilot. The brokerage house on St. James' Street was history.

He was married, at the time, to Dorothy Coulson of Ottawa. The Coulsons owned the popular Alexandra Hotel on Bank Street at Gilmour and another large hotel in Sudbury and were prominent in Ottawa social circles. Dorothy's brother, Darcy, played one season on defence with the NHL's Philadelphia Quakers in 1930–1931. In 28 games he had no goals or assists, but managed to rack up 103 penalty minutes. The remainder of his hockey career was in the Ottawa City Senior League with the Shamrocks and the Ottawa RCAF.

Johnnie persuaded his father to grubstake him, and he and his wife left Montreal and Ottawa for the mining boom in Noranda, Quebec. He set up a bush-plane airline called Commercial Airways with two planes: a Waco and a Fairchild. Dorothy was a frequent passenger on flights over the wilds of northern Quebec. His long time friend, the late Lieutenant General Reg Lane, from Victoria, British Columbia, laughed when he said that northern Quebec honed Johnnie's brawling and fighting skills.

"Johnnie was only about five feet ten inches and no

more than 160 pounds, but he loved to fight, especially when he had had a few. More than once, his pal, 'Tiny' Wilson, who was huge and weighed close to 300 pounds, would reach in and haul Johnnie out of a scrap by the back of the neck. 'Tiny' flew with Johnnie in the RCAF and, long after the war, the two of them were the original discoverers of the iron ore deposits in the Wabush area."

When war broke out in 1939, he had logged more than 482,803 kilometres in the air and, for a frustrating year and a half, the RCAF slotted the newly commissioned Johnnie Fauquier in an instructor's job teaching recruits how to fly ancient Tiger Moths. In 1941, he finally managed to wangle an overseas posting and was assigned to 405 Pathfinder Squadron as a pilot. He was 32. Johnnie had 10 to 12 years on most of his fellow bomber crews.

The legend of Johnnie Fauquier and his charmed life aloft was about to begin. His Pathfinder squadron flew Wellingtons before being assigned Halifax bombers. He flew a Halifax, then a Lancaster. He could do things with the lumbering bombers that fighter pilots could not do in a Hurricane or Spitfire. One of his favourite stunts was to sweep in so low in his Halifax that the bombardier could all but drop a two-ton bomb down a chimney.

When he switched over to high-flying Lancasters in 405 Squadron, his role was to pinpoint night targets and illuminate them with flares for the bomber stream. The average bomber was over a target, dropped his bombs, and headed home — all in three minutes. Not Johnnie Fauquier. He stayed over the target area for as long as 35 to 40 minutes leading the bomber stream in and laying more flares. When the last bomber had dropped its payload, he broke off and returned to base.

Hamburg's shipyards produced most of Germany's U-boats. Its oil refineries were vital to the Luftwaffe. It was also one of Germany's key port cities. In July 1943, Johnnie led a 700-bomber night raid on Hamburg, "Operation Gomorrah." Hamburg's assets were protected by six night-fighter bases, 22 searchlight batteries, and more than 50 heavy ack-ack guns.

Fauquier's bomber group dropped 10,000 tons of bombs on Hamburg in four nights and levelled the city. His Pathfinders lit up target areas for 1,000 bomber raids on Essen, Cologne, Berlin, and Bremen.

The main fear for a pilot of a slow-flying Lancaster was being "coned" by searchlights and raked by anti-aircraft flak (shrapnel). Fauquier solved that problem over Bremen. He used his bomber to strafe the searchlight and anti-aircraft batteries. Fauquier threw his aircraft into a steep 10,000-foot dive, levelled off just above the tree tops and his nose, tail, and mid-upper gunners raked the ground installations with a hail of lethal fire, dousing searchlights and destroying gun batteries. It was an amazing feat of flying few others would attempt with a fighter plane. Asked if he was scared, his reply was: "A man who isn't frightened lacks imagination and without imagination, he can't be a first class warrior. Let's face it: the good men were frightened, especially between briefing and takeoff. The bravest men I knew used to go to bed after briefing and refuse to eat. Sick with fear. Any man that frightened who goes to the target is brave."

A Canadian Mosquito pilot, Flying Officer William J. White, DFC, from Roland, Manitoba, flew the photo mission revealing the secret German V1 and V2 rocket base at Peenamunde on a Baltic Sea estuary. The slower, engine-driven V1 "Doodlebug" could be shot down by a fighter or tipped off course by the wing of a Hurricane or a Spitfire.

There was no defence against the V2. It was the world's first jet-guided missile and was capable of bombing London into rubble. Peenamunde had to be destroyed. On August 17, 1943, the Allies put bombers in the air to trick the Germans into believing Berlin was the target. The diversion worked; 600 heavy bombers arrived, undetected, over Peenamunde at midnight.

Fauquier's group laid down flares and he flew 17 circuits over the target, guiding the bombers in. Thirty-five minutes later, Peenamunde was wiped off the map. Laboratories and workshops were destroyed, most of the scientists were killed, and the German rocket program was history. The surprise raid was a total success, but 41 Allied bombers were destroyed.

In 1944, Johnnie was promoted to air commodore, but requested that he be demoted to his old rank of group captain so that he could continue to fly. He was given command of the RAF's elite Dambusters and he had tough acts to follow as CO: Wing Commander Guy Gibson, VC, and Wing Commander Leonard Cheshire, another Victoria Cross winner. For a Canadian to be given command of the Dambuster squadron that had blown up the Mohne and Eder dams, flooding the Ruhr Valley, was considered apostasy. To even contemplate naming a colonial as CO of the squadron that had sunk the German battleship *Tirpitz* was akin to heresy.

Tension filled the air at his first meeting with the officers of his new command. They were not impressed with his DSOs and DFC. There were a goodly number of similar "gongs" among the Dambusters. One of the Dambusters shouted out the old RAF challenge: "sing us a song or take your pants off," a favourite mess tradition to "take the mickey" out of a brass hat.

The unflappable Johnnie Fauquier dropped his pants and one of the Dambusters cooled off his hindquarters with a well-aimed stream of foamy beer. Fauquier pulled up his pants, test passed. The Dambusters then discovered he was a no-nonsense skipper: early morning callisthenics, lectures on formation flying, and shovelling snow off runways.

Johnnie Fauquier's squadron was given a new toy by Barnes Wallace, the man who designed the Wellington bomber and the bouncing bomb the Dambusters had used to destroy the Ruhr Valley dams. It was a bomb 8 metres long, weighing 10 long tons (9,979 kg), and was nicknamed "Grand Slam." Destroying key Nienburg Bridge, a vital German oil route, was "a piece of cake." Initially, he sent only four of his 18 planes in. Three direct hits took the bridge out, and the frugal Fauquier flew home with 15 Grand Slams that would fight another day.

He used them to sink Germany's last pocket battleship, the *Lutzow*, and to destroy communications and rail links. His planes dropped two Grand Slam bombs on U-boat pens near Bremen. The submarines were protected by a concrete and steel roof more than four metres thick. Grand Slams sliced through the roof as if through butter and destroyed the base. Pens at Saint-Nazaire suffered the same fate. Grand Slam was so powerful it created small earthquakes. It was dropped from high altitude and penetrated deep into the earth before it exploded. It created an underground cavern 31 metres beneath the surface. Bridges and viaducts would be shaken apart and collapse into the cavern. Bielefeld Viaduct near Bremen had been bracketed by over 3,000 tons of bombs without success. One Grand Slam dropped from 19,000 feet took out 91 metres of the viaduct.

His next targets were U-boat pens at Farge and Brest; the roofs were more than six metres of reinforced concrete. Two Grand Slams went through the roofs creating craters six metres across. The docks at Brest were heavily damaged and the heavy cruisers *Gneisenau* and *Prinz Eugen* were crippled.

The Dambusters very last operational objective was to flatten Hitler's mountain hideaway, Berchtesgaden. Unfortunately, the buildings and mountain peaks were snow covered and Fauquier's bomb aimers couldn't tell one peak from another. Their consolation prize was to level the barracks of Hitler's SS guards.

The British Navy was not convinced that the Hamburg

U-boat pens had been destroyed, so Johnnie Fauquier was ordered by Air Marshal "Bomber" Harris to eyeball them personally. The garrison at Hamburg was supposed to have surrendered. Inspecting the pens, Fauquier was surprised to find 200 German sailors at work repairing them. The commanding officer surrendered formally to Fauquier and invited him to lunch. Johnnie Fauquier became the only RCAF commander to accept a formal enemy surrender.

Johnnie Fauquier's life was on the line every time he flew into German searchlights and ack-ack flak, but he always managed to make it home. He only had one close call returning from an aborted raid over Berlin. Fauquier was over the rough North Sea, which was tossing waves 31 metres in the air, he had little or no fuel left, and his plane was icing up, when he ordered his crew to take up ditching positions.

"It was then I saw briefly one of those wonderful homing lights and made a bee-line straight for it." When he landed, the Home Guard ("Dad's army") surrounded his plane and threatened to jail the crew until they were able to prove who they were by phoning their base at Pocklington.

He minced no words describing the Berlin mission: "utterly fatigued, half frozen, and disgusted at being launched on a major operation against the German capital in weather totally unfitted to the task."

The war was over for Johnnie Fauquier. There were no brass bands to welcome Canada's most decorated airman home to Ottawa. He quietly settled into civilian life and never again took the controls of an aircraft. War had changed that. War and a long separation had also placed an irrevocable rift in his marriage, and he and his wife, Dorothy, divorced.

Reg Lane recalled that he plunged himself back into mining exploration: "Johnnie Fauquier and Tiny Wilson discovered the rich iron ore deposits of Wabush and Ungava. He was a millionaire one day and broke the next. He made and lost money more times than anyone else I ever heard of."

Johnnie Fauquier's first stiff test in civilian life came, and he flunked it. His best friend, Tiny Wilson, was killed. Tiny was a passenger in a float plane flying from Labrador to Montreal and drowned when it crashed. Johnnie was devastated and started drinking. Tiny's death hit him hard. It was the worst crisis in his life until his second wife, Mary, died from Lou Gehrig's disease in March 1980. Stories of Johnny Fauquier's "alcoholism" were greatly exaggerated. Family member, Chris Fauquier of Kanata, says "the Fauquiers were wild and loved to party, but Johnnie was never a problem drinker."

General Lane and Justice Houston both agreed: "Johnnie could be a hell-raiser at a party and try to pick a fight with someone, but he'd be bright-eyed and bushy-tailed the next morning." His second marriage to Mary Burden was the rock on which he built the rest of his life. They settled in Toronto and raised three children. Together, in partnership, they forged a successful real estate business and "Johnnie was on top again."

Three DSOs! Why not a Victoria Cross? The Fauquier

family was brought up on the folklore that he was offered the VC and declined it. "Not very likely," said General Lane, "it never happened." Since the Victoria Cross was initiated by Queen Victoria, more than 1,350 have been awarded, but only 51 have gone to airmen — 41 to Britain, four to Canada, three to Australia, two to New Zealand, and one to South Africa. Only one very junior British fighter pilot was awarded a VC in World War II.

General Lane volunteered that "early on, a very senior British air ministry officer was quoted as saying 'Canadians are not good leaders and should not be promoted beyond the rank of wing commander.' It was also a British recommendation that any VCs won by Canadian airmen should be posthumous awards," General Lane added. Indeed, the three VCs won by Canadian airmen were awarded posthumously: WO11 Andrew Charles Mynarski, RCAF; Flight Lieutenant David Ernest Hornell, RCAF; and Lieutenant Robert Hampton Gray, RCNVR. The British fighter pilot, Flight Lieutenant Eric James Brindley Nicholson, RAF Spitfire pilot, lived to display his VC and distinctive maroon ribbon.

Johnnie Fauquier's final resting place is alongside his beloved wife, Mary, on a grassy knoll in Section 51 of Beechwood Cemetery. The plain, large, grey granite grave marker simply indicates that Air Commodore John Emilius Fauquier is at rest there. Despite the many awards he received throughout his wartime career, there are no battle honours, decorations, or initials after his name.

Acknowledgments

In 1871, the editor of Nova Scotia's great *Tribune*, Joseph Howe, said "a wise nation preserves its records, gathers up its muniments, decorates the tombs of its illustrious dead, repairs its great public structures, and fosters national pride and love of country by perpetual reference to the sacrifices and glories of the past."

Canadians have paid little heed to Howe's sage advice. Our heroes are largely forgotten; the history of Canada's participation in war is treated as a form of contraband in our schools. War was never pleasant, but sometimes it was necessary in the defence of freedom and liberty. Fortunately, there are still some Canadians who remember those gallant men and women who volunteered to serve. I am grateful to them for sharing their knowledge with me.

Historian Jack Granatstein, former director of Canada's War Museum, was most helpful. Robert Hyndman and Jerry Billing were WWII Spitfire pilots who flew with Buzz Beurling. Syd Shulemson was Canada's most decorated Jewish fighter pilot and Israel's "man in Canada." He recruited Buzz Beurling to fly for Israel in 1948. Floyd Williston is a retired Manitoba deputy minister who lost two brothers who served in the RCAF in WWII. His book *Through Footless Halls* is a military classic. General Ramsey Withers is a former chief of the defence staff who served in Korea and was always available at the other end of a phone. Ottawa physician, Dr. Peter Davison, is an aviation buff whose patients include many

Acknowledgments

WWII fighter and bomber pilots. The late Ontario Justice Ed Houston was shot down in a bomber over Germany and was a prisoner of war in a German stalag. Jake Warren, former High Commissioner to Great Britain and Canadian Ambassador to the United States, served on the HMCS *Valleyfield* when she was torpedoed off Newfoundland. The family of bomber legend, Johnny Fauquier, was helpful and accommodating. Without the input of late General Reg Lane, the incredible deeds of Johnny Fauquier would have gone unrecorded. Israeli General, the late Meir Amit, former head of Mossad, was generous with his assistance. Andy MacKenzie's phenomenal memory of his two years as a prisoner of the Chinese during the Korean "police action" put flesh on the bones of an incredible story. Ontario Justice Ken Binks, Ottawa, suggested the Benny Proulx story and contributed most of the research. Mike Sheflin, Ottawa engineer and former Ottawa-Carleton transportation commissioner, provided most of the research on the sinking of the armed yacht *Raccoon* in the St. Lawrence River. His father was a victim of the torpedo from a German U-boat. The British Public Records Office at Kew, London, was always obliging.

I also owe debts of gratitude to the RAF Library, Piccadilly, London; British aviation historian Peter Elliot, London; the German Luftwaffe Historical Division, Germany's Defence Ministry; the British High Commission in Ottawa, and Israeli embassies in Ottawa and Washington.

About the Author

Pat MacAdam, a native Cape Bretoner, has made Ottawa his home since 1959. He holds degrees in arts and education from St. Francis Xavier University. He paid his way through university by writing for the *Sydney Post-Record, Halifax Chronicle-Herald,* and *Fredericton Daily Gleaner.* He spent three summers in the Canadian Officers Training Corps in Ontario and Nova Scotia, and was commissioned a lieutenant in the Royal Canadian Army Service Corps.

He was senior writer in the Public Relations Department, Expo '67, the Montreal World's Fair from 1963 to 1967. He was director of public relations and promotion for CJOH-TV and produced "Question Period" for CTV Network. He was a researcher, speechwriter, and aide to Prime Minister John Diefenbaker from 1959 to 1963. In 1983, he joined Brian Mulroney as his first employee and most senior aide. He resigned from the PM's Office in 1987 to become Minister-Counsellor, Press and Media (Press Officer) at the Canadian High Commission, Trafalgar Square, London.

His freelance writing has appeared in the Hudson's Bay Company history magazine *The Beaver, Weekend Magazine, The Canadian Magazine, Maclean's, Ottawa Citizen, Globe and Mail, National Post,* Sun Media newspapers in Ottawa and Toronto, the *Cape Bretoner Magazine,* daily newspapers in Saint John, Sydney, Halifax, Vancouver, and St. John's. His writing for the *Ottawa Citizen* earned him two National Newspaper Award nominations for excellence in feature writing.